T0276282

EXTREME | BALANCE

Paradoxical Principles
That Make You a **Champion**

BEN ASKREN | JOE DE SENA | DAVID SACKS, Ph.D.

Entrepreneur Press®

Entrepreneur Press, Publisher
Cover Design: Andrew Welyczko
Production and Composition: Mike Fontecchio, Faith & Family Publications

Library of Congress Cataloging-in-Publication Data
  Names: De Sena, Joe, 1969- author. | Askren, Ben, author. | Sacks, David
    (Sports psychologist), author.
  Title: Extreme balance : the paradoxical principles that can make you a
    champion / Joe De Sena, Spartan CEO; Ben Askren, Combat-Sport
    Champ; David Sacks, Ph.D., Sports Psychologist.
  Description: Irvine, California : Entrepreneur Press, [2024] | Includes
    index. | Summary: "Three world-class experts on performance,
    motivation, grit, and competition unveil the paradoxical principles that
    are crucial to understanding what it takes to become a champion"
    -- Provided by publisher.
  Identifiers: LCCN 2024000606 (print) | LCCN 2024000607 (ebook) | ISBN
    9781642011777 (paperback) | ISBN 9781613084878 (epub)
  Subjects: LCSH: Physical fitness. | Exercise. | Health. | Endurance sports--
    Training. | Athletics--Psychological aspects. | Mind and body.
  Classification: LCC GV481 .D4194 2024 (print) | LCC GV481 (ebook) |
    DDC 613.7--dc23/eng/20240524
  LC record available at https://lccn.loc.gov/2024000606
  LC ebook record available at https://lccn.loc.gov/2024000607

Printed in the United States of America

27 26 25 24   10 9 8 7 6 5 4 3 2 1

Table of Contents

Section I
The Hypocritical Mind:
The Data, the Science, and What We Know

Section II
The False Dichotomies:
"And" Over "Or"

Even from an early age, I could remember the lesson my dad drilled into me again and again: "It's all mental!"

I certainly didn't know what he meant at the time (aren't sports mostly physical?), but I figured he meant that if I wanted to succeed in sports, it wasn't just about strength, speed, and effort. It was about *thinking* the right way.

Soon I started reading everything I could about champions. What made them tick? What made them win? What made their mindset different from the opponents they defeated—who were often just as skilled as they were?

I obsessed over Muhammad Ali. I must've read 15 books on him. Ali wasn't just a master of the sound bite and clever quip. He was a master of the mind, constantly playing mental games with his opponents. To this day, I can't think of an athlete (or anyone!) who knew how to dig deeper than he did in the famous Thrilla in Manila bout against Joe Frazier.

I also obsessed about becoming a champion in the sport I drifted toward: wrestling. While I played all sports as a child, I came to love wrestling. It was a place where I could control my destiny: just me, my opponent, and the mat.

Wrestling wasn't just about takedowns and reversals. It was a battle of wills, and I loved the solo journey of preparing for the matches that lasted no longer than 6 minutes.

When I got into high school, I started exploring the field of psychology even more so I could teach myself to think as effectively as possible for my wrestling matches. But after I earned a scholarship to the University of Missouri, I grew more and more critical of the sports-psychology books I was reading.

They told you *how* to think, but they never explained that the brain is a confusing and complex place where conflicting ideas, values, opinions, and thoughts battled against each other, with no referee present to hold high the arm of the winner. And those conflicts and contradictions can be both a blessing and a curse.

Being stubborn can help you dedicate yourself to training, but it can also prevent you from being open to new ideas that will help you develop. Being obsessive can help you pay attention to the details that make you elite, but it can also force you to think so much that anxiety hampers your performance. Being tough can help you power through the pain, but it can also cause you great harm (uh, maybe don't compete with four stress fractures?).

When I was a junior at Mizzou, a woman named Renee Mapes was earning her sport psychology PhD there, and she had to work with a team as part of her program. I talked to her frequently because I had so many questions about sport psych, and I was trying to achieve the optimal mindset.

Over the next year, we bounced ideas off each other, and I got inspired to pursue the field even further by taking quite a few graduate-level courses in sport psychology. Those experiences laid the foundation for this book.

In my last two years at Mizzou, I went 87-0 with two national titles and two Dan Hodge Trophies, awarded to the best college wrestler in the U.S. Something was clearly working, and it wasn't just what was happening on the mat; it was what was happening in my mind.

As I trained for the Olympics and started my mixed martial arts career, my passion for sport psychology never went away. That's about the time I started formulating the idea that would eventually become the core of this book:

How do we balance the many mindsets that appear to be in direct opposition to one another?

During this same time, I started the Askren Wrestling Academy with my brother, Max, and my high school coach, John Mesenbrink. There, I started to apply my thoughts on sport psych to not only myself but also to the athletes I was coaching. (In 2023, we had an NCAA champion, a U20 world champion, and five other national champions.)

In 2021 I appeared on Spartan founder Joe De Sena's podcast *The Hard Way*. Among other things, I mentioned the theory I was working on and where I thought the available sport psych books were lacking. A lot of my ideas really meshed with Joe's Spartan Way. He connected me with sport psychologist David Sacks, and we began digging into the guts of this book. David has really made this theory come to life, and together the three of us have created a book that clearly lays it out for you to follow.

I have seen over the years that many of my athletes value certain mental characteristics over others. They can neglect some really important aspects because they like the other side of the equation more.

But if you can find EXTREME BALANCE, you will create a mindset that will allow you to perform at truly elite levels.

—Ben Askren,
2008 Olympic wrestling team member
and two-time NCAA national champion

The Paradoxical Quest
for Extreme Balance

In just about any sport, a strong stance is vital.

Stand with your feet apart, keep your weight on your toes, bend your knees slightly, and keep your head up. In this way, you are ready to move in any direction and react to anything that comes your way. You've put yourself in the best possible position to succeed. You're prepared for the unknown.

Athletes spend a lot of time thinking about and perfecting a solid stance—so much so that it becomes habit and the foundation for every move we make. While we put a lot of effort into our physical stance, however, most of us ignore our mental stance. The way we treat our mental positioning is like standing on one foot with our hands tied behind our back and our eyes closed. In this stance, we're ready for nothing, and the unknown will chew us up, spit us out, and then go back for seconds.

But that's what so many of us do. We adopt a system of values and way of thinking, and we develop an obsessive mindset that becomes "who we are," and we never allow ourselves to deviate from that, even when it would help us. If you think of yourself as a perfectionist, you always must be one. If you compete through pain, you must do it every time. If you have an ego the size of Canada, then you damn well must never display an ounce of vulnerability.

But this one-way street of thinking is exactly the thing that's working against you. It's the psychological equivalent of an unbalanced stance. Throughout this book, in contrast, we'll explain how to develop Extreme Balance in your mental stance, so that you'll be prepared to shift from one mindset to another and to adapt your psychological approach based on the situation at hand.

Your strengths—in certain circumstances—can become your shortcomings, and unless you can see your way past them, your defeats will outnumber your victories. If you refuse to accept that there will always be unknowns, that obsessive mindset that has helped you so much in your training will become a major liability.

Any soldier will tell you that unforeseen events happen in combat *and* leading up to it (whether it's getting clipped by a bullet you didn't see coming or suffering a freak injury in training). In those moments, the key to your success lies in how you respond. Will you panic? Or will you accept the new status quo and proceed from there? Do you say "Oh crap" or "OK"? If it's the former, you're in for a tough time. If it's the latter, you're still in for a tough time, but you'll have the skills to adapt on the fly. To quote the informal slogan of the U.S. Marine Corps, you'll "improvise, adapt, and overcome."

That's what Extreme Balance is all about: accepting that your approach to situations should be flexible. Your mental stance needs to set you up to be ready to handle anything.

Often, aspiring champions seek the advice of coaches and respected mentors, hoping someone will have the key to success— the mental roadmap to victory. Unfortunately, you often get conflicting advice—and that can throw you off balance. One successful coach says, "You should play to win, not lose." Another, who has equally impressive credentials, says, "You must hate losing more than you love winning."

The confusion lies not in the fact that people offer different advice; it's that the world of coaching, training, and mentoring can often feel like a whirlwind of contradictions. One moment, you're told you must pay attention to the details to succeed (it's the difference between good and great!). In the next, you're told you're thinking too damn much and you just need to relax.

Even the clearest advice, delivered in the most concrete terms from the most respected elders, is unreliable. How, then, can you know what to believe? Or think? Or do? How can you cultivate the mindset of a winner and use the necessary tools, strategies, and mental mastery to succeed at whatever you want in life?

The Spartan truth is that there is no secret recipe. Except for this: When faced with a choice of one approach, mindset, or attitude vs. another, frequently the best option is not to choose sides. The best answer is to find a balance between these two opposite ways of thinking.

This is Extreme Balance, and it is the paradoxical way of thinking that can give you a winning mentality.

It is tempting to seek the "best" way of thinking and adopt a clear-cut approach to apply in every situation. If this were possible, then achieving success would be easy. Yet the Spartan Way is not an easy way, and the path to excellence is not a simple one. The Spartan Way requires commitment, passion, self-awareness, and discipline. It requires ongoing efforts to make improvements over time, and this includes continuously adapting your mentality to what is needed in a given moment.

7

It's not about training too hard or training too little. It's not about respecting your opponents or wanting to crush them. It's not about using your brain or using your instincts. It's not about being confident or being insecure.

In fact, the first thing you need to do is eliminate the word "or" from your mindset and substitute "and." Of course, altering your approach isn't as easy as changing one word and embracing the power of "and." Change is not simple.

While it's tempting to hope for an easy formula for success, that hope will actually lead you in the opposite direction. When you adhere rigidly to a set of rules, your stubbornness can result in poor performance. For example, "no pain, no gain" can lead you to aggravate a minor injury that could have healed with rest. And an "always go on offense" mentality can result in a loss to an otherwise beatable opponent who happens to have a solid defense for your best attacks. It's tempting to embrace simple instructions that you can faithfully follow to a championship, but no such thing exists. Rules that work brilliantly in one situation can lead you astray in another.

This is Extreme Balance.

Just as it takes thousands of hours of practice to master a physical skill, so, too, does it take thousands of hours to hone your mental game. You do it by observing the experts, by listening to people you respect, by focusing on your mental strength as you train physically, and, yes, by reading. None of these things, done on their own or just once or twice, will ensure your success. Developing a winner's mindset is a career-long process.

In today's influencer-laden world, there are thousands of people touting their "foolproof" (yet unproven) recipes to achieve greatness, success, or wealth. And yet, even with all their "answers," we're still living in a world of high stress, complete burnout, and psychological struggles. The more we think we're solving problems, the more we're exacerbating them.

It's not easy to be a Spartan.

But if you are willing to put in the work and take the time to navigate the nuances and apparent contradictions of a champion, you can become one.

Looking in Dark Places

In *Extreme Balance*, we'll give you some essential principles to guide you in your ongoing quest to improve. We won't tell you *what* to think but rather give you a framework for *how* to think about your psychological approach to life's many forms of combat and performance.

We'll cover strategies for finding balance between two extremes, switching from one mentality to another, and holding competing ideals in your mind. (Putting these principles into practice is up to you.)

Think of this book as you might think of going to a summer training camp. You want a camp with a quality staff and a proven track record of success, and you can expect to learn—or at least be exposed to—solid skills and techniques. But whether you actually use those skills and techniques in competition the following season depends on what you do when the camp is over. How much you benefit by reading these pages depends on what you do with the information after you finish the book. We will provide you with the building blocks for a winner's mentality and for training and competing the Spartan Way. We hope you put that information to good use.

There's an old joke that illustrates our mission here. A man is walking through a dark alley and realizes he's lost his keys. In his distress, he walks toward a streetlight and begins searching the ground. Another man walks up and asks what he's doing.

"I'm looking for my keys," the first man says. "I lost them somewhere in the alley."

"Well, if you lost them in the alley, why are you looking for them here?" the other man asks.

The first man looks up and says, "Because the light is better here."

The quest for a champion's mentality is similar. It's tempting to look where it's easy to see, but the journey is challenging and often confusing, loaded with paradoxes and contradictions. If you want to figure things out, you've got to persevere in the dark alleys.

In this book, we'll walk you through the various mental skills and psychological principles needed to perform at the highest level and explain how top performers integrate seemingly incompatible mindsets to adapt to a situation's demands. For example, we'll cover how to remain humble and coachable even as you exude extreme confidence, how to impose your will on your opponent even as you adjust your game plan, and how to maintain your hatred of failure and a burning drive to pursue the toughest challenges.

In practice, when you have two extreme principles, people think they always have to lean into the "side" they value most. But you can use these extreme sides in three ways (and this changes based on situations and circumstances):

1. Find a spot in the middle of the two extremes (for example, feeling moderately excited going into a competition – not too relaxed nor too nervous)
2. Flip-flop between the two extremes (for example, believing you need to get better during training and that you're the best when competing)

3. Hold onto the two extremes simultaneously (for example, being furious at a training partner, but still loving and respecting them)

You'll see how this plays out in many different ways as we break down some of the more common mental conflicts competitors face.

We've written this book chiefly for those Spartans devoted to mastering the mental side of performance. It's also a valuable volume for those who help others achieve excellence, including coaches, trainers, parents, and counselors. Many of the examples relate to individual sports—especially combat sports—though the principles and concepts are relevant for all types of high performers, including athletes and non-athletes alike.

Importantly, we have the track record to back up the guidance we offer. Our team includes:

- Ben Askren, a champion in multiple combat sports and one of the most decorated American wrestlers of the past several decades. Known as a creative innovator, Ben is also the leader of a highly successful wrestling training academy and has coached multiple state, national, and world champions.

- Joe De Sena, an accomplished athlete and leader, having completed legendary feats as an endurance and adventure racer and as the founder and CEO of Spartan. In addition to his individual accomplishments, he is well on his way to getting 100 million people off their couches and into a physically and emotionally healthy lifestyle, the Spartan Way.

- Dr. David Sacks, a clinical and sport psychologist and former college athlete who has helped thousands of clients achieve success across a broad range of performance domains.

In addition to our own expertise, we have interviewed many elite performers and coaches, who have agreed to share their knowledge and guidance with you here. Just as these winners constantly work on honing their techniques, so too are they working to hone their mindset every day. Their input, combined with the scientific underpinnings we describe, provides you with thorough (if not always simple) explanations of the psychological principles that will set you up for success.

In This Book

As we'll advise throughout the book, we want you to use the salt *and* the pepper. The same person who advocates for one approach may, in another situation, sincerely extol the virtues of its opposite. The well-informed expert realizes that the paradoxical approach often is the very thing that *works*.

The lessons here go beyond picking an approach that works best for you; we suggest rather adapting your approach to the situation at hand. This requires open-mindedness and flexibility, as well as a willingness to change when things aren't working and accept that your pursuit of excellence is a work in progress.

Here's how we'll get there:

- **Section I**: We cover what we know from science and practice about the paradoxical aspects of performance. We outline several areas in which dual mechanisms operate simultaneously and explain why both are needed to sustain excellence. We also explore the role of art and science in becoming a champion, the importance of holding the tension of opposites, and the risk of being inflexible and overcommitted to one side of the coin. This section does a deep dive into the concepts and strategies of working hard, working smart, and devoting thousands of hours to deliberate practice, which is what makes people into champions.

- **Section II**: By examining eight "false dichotomies" that competitors commonly face, we'll show you how to put the principles from Section I into practice. Each chapter begins with an infographic highlighting the pros and cons of each side, as well as guidance on when to lean one way or the other. You'll also hear from various champions in sports and other walks of life, as they share their views on seeming contradictions, such as exuding supreme confidence while remaining humble, imposing your will while adapting to your adversary, and being both independent and a team member, among many others.

We'll conclude by describing the myriad ways that lessons learned through sport and combat translate into success in life (and the few ways in which they don't).

We can't guarantee that you'll win every time. You can't excel at something just by reading about it, but these pages contain the building blocks you need for success, with many champions telling you in their own words how they've used those blocks to get to where they are today.

The first step on this path to excellence is understanding that it may initially seem that the "paradox" of balancing opposing approaches is an obstacle to your success. In fact, it's the exact opposite.

That is the truth behind Extreme Balance and the path to becoming a champion.

The Hypocritical Mind:
The Data, the Science,
and What We Know

— CHAPTER 1 —

Where Salt Meets Pepper

"The more you know, the harder you will find it
To make up your mind.
It doesn't really matter if you find
You can't see which grass is greener.
Chances are it's neither,
And either way it's easier
To see the difference
When you're sitting on the fence."

—Australian comedian and musician Tim Minchin, "The Fence"

All too often we find ourselves facing fabricated choices. Sweet or salty? Fast or slow? Offense or defense? Grappling or striking? Art or science? Student or athlete? These are false dichotomies. Although they're often presented as opposites that require us to choose one or the other, there's no good reason we can't choose both—or choose one now and the other at a different time.

The natural world "knows" this. If you look at any area of science, you're likely to find multiple and often competing mechanisms interacting to make things work. Within our own bodies, several such dualisms are continually working together to keep us going. Our nervous system, for example, includes both sympathetic and parasympathetic components.

The sympathetic system is responsible for the "fight or flight" response and helps us spring into action when we're threatened. The parasympathetic system, in contrast, helps us settle down and relax when the threat has passed.

If the sympathetic system overreacts, perhaps by perceiving a threat where there isn't one, the parasympathetic system can take over and calm us down. The parasympathetic system also does this after an actual threat is gone, lowering our heart rate and respiration, restoring resting blood flow, and reducing muscle tension. This is sometimes called the "rest and digest" response. Though it would get you killed if an enemy threatens, it's the perfect way to simmer down when the coast is clear. It's also useful when you need to conserve energy for a sustained challenge, such as a daylong competition.

Of the two systems, it would be foolish to ask, "Which is better?" Both are essential for our survival. A better question is, "Which is needed right now?"

That question, it turns out, is one of the main themes of this book.

Fortunately for us, that question is usually answered automatically. That's because these two systems are both part of our autonomic nervous system, which operates without the need for conscious control. If we had to concentrate on keeping our heart beating and breathing in and out and digesting our food all the time, we'd be overwhelmed. In a state of nature, we wouldn't survive very long. And herein lies another duality: the autonomic and somatic, or voluntary, nervous systems. While the autonomic system operates on its own, the somatic nervous system requires deliberate decision making, such as choosing to move our legs and arms. Again, both systems are essential, and we thrive when our internal state matches the demands of the situation. (We will explore these two systems further in Chapter 10.)

To dive even deeper, let's look at another dualism embedded in the sympathetic response. Which is better: fight or flight?

Some will automatically say "Fight!"

That may be true in many cases. But fighting every time makes you predictable and easy to manipulate. It also tires you out. If you find you've brought a knife to a gunfight, staying in the fight will get you shot. Better to run. Or you might be in a fistfight in the cage or ring when your tiring opponent musters one last surge and tries to swarm you. The smarter move at that moment would be to evade—you'd be choosing flight so you could continue to fight at another time.

Being overcommitted to any one way of doing things leads to all kinds of mistakes, especially when the current situation suggests another way would be better. There's nothing wrong with having a preferred way of doing things. But if that's the only way you know, or the only way you're willing to try, someone is going to figure that out and use it against you. A true Spartan is not confined by a commitment to a single way of approaching a task or working through a challenge. Spartans use any tools at their disposal to work toward a goal, and this means drawing on multiple inputs.

We therefore shouldn't ask whether it's better to get psyched up or stay relaxed before a competition, or whether we should focus on offensive or defensive strategies, or whether it's better to be an individual or a team player.

Instead, we ought to practice both approaches and get used to transitioning from one to the other. Keep this importance of dualism in mind the next time you're frustrated with a coach or a teacher who stresses the importance of a specific quality one day and promotes the opposite concept the next. Although they might seem to be contradicting themselves, they're likely showing you both aspects of an important duality.

A Multidimensional View

Very often, we mistakenly look at dual mechanisms as the opposite ends of a single spectrum. We depict this in Figure 1.1 on page 22, where a single line indicates the amount of some characteristic a person has. If we were measuring their height, weight, or strength on the bench press, this would be an accurate way to view it. When looking at a dualism, though, we'd be missing an important part of the picture.

Unlike height or weight or speed, which are variables that can be measured on a single dimension, most of our behavioral and psychological tendencies result from multiple inputs and processes. If we're looking at someone's level of arousal at a given moment, we know from the brief explanation above that it's determined by inputs from the sympathetic and parasympathetic nervous systems. These dual processes drive all sorts of actions, and we'll be exploring many of the resulting dichotomies throughout the following chapters.

To illustrate these dual mechanisms, the second figure shows two vertical lines, indicating that, when we see a person exhibit behavioral or psychological tendencies, it is the result of their status on two separate variables. In this case, the figure depicts an athlete with a very high level of excitement and a moderate level of relaxation. If you didn't know them well, you might describe them as slightly excited, though a more accurate description is that they are usually super-excited and have learned to moderate this tendency by adding relaxation skills. They can now be both excited and relaxed at the same time.

Many other variables fit this model as well. You might think of introversion and extroversion as opposite ends of a spectrum, yet many people describe themselves as both. At any given moment, then, you can think of being on a range from high to low on introversion, while also being high to low on extroversion.

Another example is your motivation to win and your motivation to avoid losing. Rarely are we completely motivated by one and not at all motivated by the other. You can look at being offensive or defensive the same way. You don't have to choose one or the other as your guiding principle. Instead, you can work to build your skills at both, which gives you the flexibility to navigate between these options as the situation requires, making you a much more formidable competitor. Flexibility is a critical physical quality, and it's equally (if not more) important as a psychological quality. Conversely, being closed-minded or extremist in your thinking will limit your development at best and lead to danger and pathology at worst. We will look at these concepts in the next chapter.

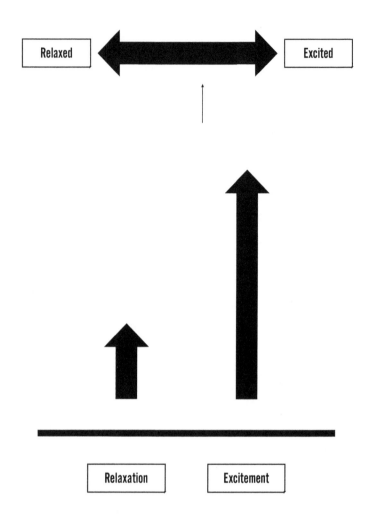

Figure 1.1: Unidimensional And Multidimensional Views.
Two ways of conceptualizing a person's behavior. The top figure assumes one variable, with an individual landing along a single spectrum. The bottom figure assumes dual mechanisms operating in concert, with an individual possessing different amounts of each.

— CHAPTER 2 —

The Problem with Extremism

"Everything in moderation, including moderation."

—Oscar Wilde

Passion, by most accounts, is a good thing. Passion can lift you to new heights and help you overcome obstacles that would derail your competitors. And if you're a champion—or on your way to becoming one—then you clearly have passion.

Passion—and its cousin, commitment—is a necessary ingredient for developing a winning mindset. But like all good things, it can have its downside. For example, when you have no flexibility and stubbornly stick to a certain way of operating, your passion can counterpunch your goals right in the jaw.

Generally, the mindset of "if something is good, more must be better" is misguided. More examples:

- **Confidence**: You want to believe you can win. But when confidence becomes overconfidence, you can underestimate your opponents and mistakenly think you don't need to try as hard.

23

- **Respect**: You should respect your opponents, but too much respect can lead to fear and hesitation.
- **Rigor in training**: You know how it is: never cut corners, get the right amount of sleep, and stick to a diet. Being obsessive about training helps you develop habits that, over time, lead to better performance. But taken to the extreme, it becomes obsessive-compulsive disorder (OCD), where the person can't function unless they do everything in a certain way and any change in routine leads to severe anxiety.

Extreme virtues can morph into destructive vices. An ideal champion has a healthy mindset and a strong belief in themselves. They think they're great at their chosen endeavor, aren't afraid to say it, and don't let anyone get in their way. If someone tries, they'll muster all their resources to beat them back and emerge victorious.

But what happens when you take that attitude to the extreme? You get narcissistic personality disorder, which refers to someone who has a pervasive pattern of grandiosity, a constant need for admiration, and a lack of empathy for others. (We all know people who think they're great, need others to know it, and always take care of themselves first.)

But where's the line? Maybe it's when a healthy self-belief turns into you not recognizing your own weaknesses and refusing to accept a coach pointing out your flaws. But if you have a robust but nonpathological level of self-esteem, you'll crave critical feedback because you believe you have what it takes to turn your weaknesses into strengths.

The goal here is not to warn you against any particular characteristic but rather for you to recognize that taking any characteristic to the extreme can backfire. Being completely self-absorbed is a problem, but so is being completely selfless, which at the extreme can manifest as dependent personality disorder: someone who is submissive, clingy, and so invested in making sure others are OK that they often volunteer for unpleasant tasks to gain their approval. These "martyrs" or "people pleasers" often get taken advantage of by narcissists.

You don't have to give up being selfless; just use it in moderation. Your goal should be to land somewhere between narcissist and doormat.

Even when someone wants to move more toward the center after realizing they're too extreme, it's often hard to do because they fear going too far toward the opposite extreme. A narcissist fears that acknowledging a flaw means admitting they're worthless. An extremely humble person worries that acknowledging their strengths means they're being arrogant.

Likewise, the offensive-minded competitor feels timid when playing defense. And the rule follower feels like they're cheating when pushing the bounds of legality in a contest, even when all the other competitors are doing it and the referees are calling things loosely. When your stance has become extreme, the causes are often twofold. First, you highly value the characteristic you've adopted, and second, you demonize the opposite characteristic. So in order to move away from your extremist tendencies, you will have to accept a moderate level of the quality you have previously disdained. In doing so, you may feel like you are violating your own principles.

Keep in mind, though, we're not advising a drastic change—just a nudge toward the center, like scooting from the 99th to the 95th percentile. That may not sound like a big ask, measured against the population as a whole. But you aren't the population, and when you've spent your whole life cultivating a particular way of operating, downshifting a few percentile points is a huge change internally.

Figure 2.1 on page 27 illustrates this concept. The larger curve on top represents the entire population's attitudes on a specific variable, in this case "risk-taking." People range from low to high on this, with those farthest to the left having the lowest tolerance for risk—the kind of people who never venture beyond their comfort zone. Those farthest to the right on the large curve are the daredevils. They will try anything and accept any challenge, consequences be damned. It goes without saying that Spartans tend to be on the right-hand side of the curve.

The smaller curve on the bottom represents an extreme risk-taker's place on the curve. At the highest end of their range, they're as much of a risk-taker as anyone. At the lowest end of their personal range, they're still in the upper 95 percent or so of risk-takers in the population. Let's suppose that they've taken ill-advised risks that have led to injuries (sparring with much bigger teammates without using protective gear, for example). Our prospective champion would be wise to scale back to the lowest end of their range, yet to them, this would feel like cowardice, as they have only known the daredevil's experience. In their case, they need to learn to tolerate that feeling, because it will help them take appropriate risks without the downside of extremism.

Risk-Taking Distribution

Figure 2.1: Risk-Taking Ranges for the Population and an Individual Extreme Risk-Taker. The larger curve above shows the distribution of risk-taking in the population. The smaller curve below shows the personal range for a single high-level risk-taker relative to the population.

It's also difficult for a champion to act more like a normal person than an extremist because, by definition, a champion is not normal. They have risen to the top of the podium by being more committed and working harder than others.

We should be clear here: The goal is not to be normal. The goal is to be abnormal without being pathological.

Sure, there are times when an extreme response is called for, but you need to understand the conditions under which that holds true. Going all out and throwing a knockout punch has its place, but if your only option is the big swing, that leaves you vulnerable in other ways.

In performance psychology studies, one of the most robust findings is that people perform best at a moderate level of arousal/anxiety. Too little anxiety and you're not motivated enough to focus and step up your game. Too much anxiety and you're at risk of choking. Thus, a moderate level tends to be ideal.

In sport psychology circles, this concept is captured in the "inverted U curve" (shown in Figure 2.2 below). This phenomenon is also known as the Yerkes-Dodson law, named for the researchers who first studied it. Robert Yerkes and John Dillingham Dodson found that laboratory mice mastered a task most effectively and quickly when stressed at a moderate level, a finding that has been replicated among other species, including humans.

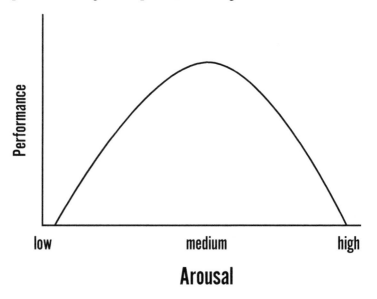

Figure 2.2: The "Inverted-U" Relationship between Arousal and Performance.
At low levels of arousal, performance tends to be low. With increased arousal, performance improves, up to an optimal point at the height of the curve. Beyond that point, if arousal continues to increase, performance declines through "choking" under the pressure.

A prevailing explanation for the phenomenon is known as cue utilization theory, which proposes that people have a limited capacity for attention, and the more aroused or anxious we are, the fewer things we can attend to. When you're relaxed, you pay attention to cues that matter to your performance, as well as to things that are irrelevant. In this state, a coach might admonish you to get your head in the game. When your anxiety level increases, your focus narrows until, at some optimal point (the top of the curve), you're paying attention to all the relevant cues and none of the possible distractions. But when you're extremely anxious, your focus is so narrow that you can't take in even the basic information that you need, and you choke. You forget how much time is left or fail to notice the defender who picks off your pass or neglect some other important aspect of your game that you would have handled better if you'd been more relaxed.

So you should generally aim for a moderate level of arousal.

The trick is that the ideal level is different for each person. Your ideal number of butterflies in your stomach will be different from your teammate's. In addition, your optimal state will change over time and depending on the task at hand. If you're competing in a powerlifting competition, you're likely to do well by getting pumped up, maybe even by smacking yourself in the head. But when you're playing quarterback and tracking five receivers and the defense, you'll be much better off taking some deep breaths before the play. Thus, a quarterback's optimal level of arousal is going to be lower than the optimal level for a powerlifter.

Because competition requires an array of skills and knowledge, hyperfocusing on one particular aspect means you risk neglecting other important facets of your craft—another danger of an extremist mindset. A common example, especially among combat-sport athletes, is placing your toughness on a pedestal. Whether it's rooted in the culture of the sport or a misguided attempt to prove how much of a badass they are, many aspiring champions regard toughness as the only metric of their worth. As a result, they will always choose the most difficult (or *toughest*) course of action.

It's true that shying away from the required hard work of training or folding when things get challenging will prevent you from becoming the best you can be. But if there is both a difficult and an easier path to success available to you, the wise choice is to take the easier path. There's no reason to get beaten up on the way to victory if you can win without taking damage. Even if you are tough enough to win a point or a round in the most difficult way, do it in the most efficient way instead. Conserve your energy and your body for the long haul.

In prioritizing toughness above all else, you minimize other important qualities required to be a champion, one of which is intelligence. Woe to the athlete who neglects smart decision making. In doing so, they often make dumb choices, such as repeating the same technique that's not working or ignoring an injury until what could have been a treatable problem leads to long-term harm.

Such decisions might be the tough guy's path, but they're also stupid. As former Stanford wrestling coach Chris Horpel teaches, the best route is to shun this tough-stupid behavior and instead adopt a tough-smart approach, where you leverage both your toughness and your intelligence to pursue your goals. This is shown in Figure 2.3 below, where any action can be classified as either tough or wimpy, while also being categorized as smart or stupid. Obviously, you want to stay in the tough-smart quadrant on the upper right.

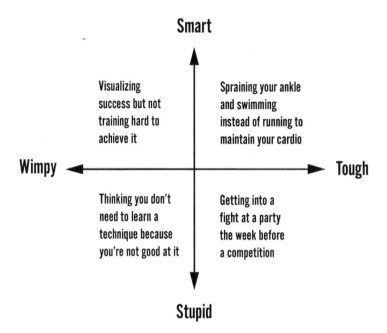

Smart

Wimpy ← → **Tough**

Visualizing success but not training hard to achieve it

Spraining your ankle and swimming instead of running to maintain your cardio

Thinking you don't need to learn a technique because you're not good at it

Getting into a fight at a party the week before a competition

Stupid

Figure 2.3: The Tough-Smart Mentality.
The "tough-smart" quadrant shows that both toughness and intelligence factor into effective decision making.

The most common reason for neglecting important considerations like intelligence or efficiency is having something to prove to yourself about whatever quality you've placed on a pedestal. This is different from wanting to prove your doubters wrong. Needing to prove something to yourself is born of self-doubt. Remember, if you know you're tough, you don't have to go out of your way to prove it. You'll show your toughness when you need to, but you won't make things harder than they need to be. The more confident you are, the less you'll let your inner battles distract from the actual battles with your opponents.

The tough-stupid trap is just one of the ways this overcommitment to one quality can play out. Sometimes people focus so much on physical strength that they neglect flexibility, or they prioritize perfect technique at the expense of conditioning.

A true winner is committed to excellence in all aspects of their chosen domain, not just one. Extremism in one aspect is a threat to the others. It can lead to stubbornness, which in turn leads to a lack of flexibility, another important characteristic of a champion and one we'll be discussing in the next chapter.

CHAPTER 3

The Importance of Flexibility

*"A foolish consistency is the hobgoblin of little minds, adored by
little statesmen and philosophers and divines. With consistency
a great soul has simply nothing to do. He may as well concern
himself with his shadow on the wall. Speak what you think now in
hard words, and to-morrow speak what to-morrow thinks in hard
words again, though it contradict every thing you said to-day."*

—American essayist and philosopher Ralph Waldo Emerson, "Self-Reliance"

Outliers—as you may know from a statistics class, a bestselling
book, or your own observations—are data points that, well,
defy logic.

They're outliers because they're vastly different from what you
believe to be true based on your data or experience; we see outliers
in all aspects of life—sports, business, education, government,
families.

Take school, for example. Looking at the correlation between
IQ and course grades, the kids with the highest IQs tend to have
the highest grades, those with the lowest IQ scores have the lowest
grades, and those with average IQ scores have average grades.
Makes sense.

This allows you to predict a kid's grades (with reasonable accuracy) based on their score on an IQ test. But you also might find that a couple of kids defy this prediction. There could be a student with low IQ scores who has some of the highest grades in their class, or someone with a super high IQ who is failing all their classes. They're outliers.

In another correlational study you might be looking at athleticism (which you assess through a combination of strength, speed, endurance, and flexibility) and win-loss records in a sport. You would likely find a positive correlation between athleticism and the percentage of wins, meaning that the more athletic someone is, the better their win-loss record. But here again, you very well may find that some athletes do far better or worse than their numbers would predict.

So what do outliers have to do with becoming a winner? Though they skew statistical results and frustrate theorists and researchers alike, outliers are quite useful because they show the exceptions to the rule, where our theories don't apply. They have a pesky way of showing up everywhere, and they can make life complicated, especially if you like operating with hard and fast rules. Outliers can right hook your rulebook right out of the ring. They show that rules may work most of the time, but not all the time. And if you're paying attention, they can teach you that adapting your approach when you face a new situation can help you even when your strategy has always worked before. Outliers show us that exceptions should be part of our rules.

If your job is deciding who to admit to your college, for example, you can use students' test scores to make an educated guess about how they would do, but you'll get it wrong some of the time. You'll admit some really "smart" kids who fail out and reject some with low test scores who go on to do great things elsewhere. Likewise, if you're a scout for a professional sports team and rely only on athletes' performance in a combine assessment—where they run sprints, lift weights, and jump to show their core athleticism—you'll miss out on the outliers, who will either miserably disappoint or greatly exceed expectations.

Tom Brady, by consensus the best professional quarterback of the modern era, was the 199th player (and seventh quarterback) selected in the 2000 National Football League draft. His relatively poor performance at the NFL combine and lack of traditional athletic traits belied the "intangible" qualities that make him a true outlier. It took a coach like the Patriots' Bill Belichick, who was willing to look beyond the numbers, to give the future legend a chance.

While there may be any number of ways people become outliers, our beliefs, rules, and strategies are fallible. Even when we think we've got it all figured out, there's always a chance that the exception *works*, and we have to be willing to change to push past our perceived limits.

While there are plenty of areas where formulas work just fine (math and baking come to mind), the human element means there are no dependable algorithms in most life situations (and certainly not in sports, where there's an opponent trying to beat you).

The closest alternative is to use what's known as a heuristic. Unlike the strict formula of an algorithm, a heuristic is more like a "rule of thumb." If you follow a heuristic, you're very likely (but not guaranteed) to get a positive result. A common heuristic in daily life is the "retrace your steps" approach to find your lost wallet or keys. In sports, a heuristic would be training like crazy to be in better shape than your competitors and then using your superior conditioning to push the pace until, inevitably, your opponents wear down and you can exert your will over them. This is an excellent heuristic. If you have the toughness and work ethic to follow it, you'll be victorious most of the time—but not all the time. Sooner or later, you'll run into an outlier who falls outside the limits of your heuristic. This doesn't mean you should abandon an approach that works for you most of the time; rather, you should remain open-minded and flexible enough to adapt when the situation requires it. It's like the "pirate's code" from the Pirates of the Caribbean movies. As Barbossa says in *The Curse of the Black Pearl*, "The code is more what you'd call guidelines than actual rules."

In sports, we encounter many "hard-and-fast" rules, such as:

- In wrestling, never cross your feet and always keep your head up.
- In boxing, never drop your hands.
- In tennis, always go for the highest percentage shot.

These are essential rules, but they all have exceptions. In fact, some of the greatest advances in sports have come from athletes who have broken the rules. Their approach seemed radical at the time, but they made it work, and their success changed the game.

Dick Fosbury won a gold medal in the high jump at the 1968 Olympics using a technique no one had ever seen before, one that has since been named for him—the "Fosbury Flop." The revolutionary approach of going backward over the bar was made possible by enhancements to the landing pad, which allowed for techniques that would have previously led to severe injuries. Fosbury used those changes and came up with a creative solution that eventually became standard practice for the next generation of high jumpers.

John Smith, a six-time wrestling world champion (including two Olympic gold medals) and former head wrestling coach at Oklahoma State University from 1992 to 2024, invented the "John Smith single leg" takedown. (When you're an effective rule-breaking innovator, you get a technique named after you.) Also known simply as a "low single," Smith's technique involves getting extremely low and grasping your opponent's leg at the calf or even at the foot. It requires you to reach a bit with your arm and get your torso and head low, which previously was considered poor technique. But Smith broke these rules and excelled by doing so. He effectively pursued a part of his opponents' bodies (their lower legs) that were previously not considered viable targets of attack, and which they were unaccustomed to defending. John's willingness to defy convention led to a new era in the sport. What was previously viewed as wrong became another way to get it right.

Ben Askren, a wrestler who similarly showed flexibility in his thinking to solve problems and evolve the sport, was an expert at "scrambling." This changed what had previously been a defensive tactic into a counter-offensive weapon. Rather than blindly subscribing to the prevailing wisdom of the sport, he creatively used his particular set of skills to succeed in a new manner, making "funky" a legitimate way to win.

These athletes illustrate the power of creativity, flexibility, and a willingness to adapt to the environment.

Just as physical flexibility gives you an enhanced range of motion and lets you compete from a greater number of positions, mental flexibility allows you to take advantage of a vast array of approaches, techniques, and styles.

We can see this in the evolution of mixed martial arts. Though MMA is a relatively young sport, it has progressed through multiple phases. In its earliest days, MMA fighters were largely out to prove that their chosen arts were the best. Boxers boxed, Thai fighters struck with knees and elbows, and jujitsu players looked for submissions. Everyone was a specialist who tried to execute their unique game plan.

Soon, fighters realized they needed to learn something about their opponents' arts. A striker had to learn some grappling—if only to know how to defend against it. Grapplers had to learn to strike and to defend against striking attacks. Still, most were relying on their original backgrounds to win.

Eventually, people began training as true mixed martial artists, rather than as a specific type of martial artist competing under mixed rules. Though a fighter may have a core base or preferred style, anyone who hopes to succeed at MMA must be competent in a range of styles and be open and flexible in their thinking. As Miyamoto Musashi wrote in *The Book of Five Rings*, they must "become acquainted with every art [and] know the ways of all professions."

In this way, the true mixed martial artist represents a person who is culturally competent. Rather than being shut off to ways of doing things that don't fit their preferred model, they remain open to other viewpoints and incorporate them into their psyche. If others do things differently, they are curious to learn why, and they actively seek out alternative approaches. They minimize their biases and judge other approaches on their effectiveness, rather than on a preconceived notion of there being only one right way.

This concept of mental flexibility represents a major aspect of our character. In the field of personality, psychologists have found that our character traits can be classified into five major categories. One of these is called "Openness to Experience" or simply "Openness." (The others are Neuroticism, Extroversion, Agreeableness, and Conscientiousness.)

Those of us with high levels of Openness are curious about ourselves and others and generally lead lives that are richer in experience. In contrast, people with low levels of Openness tend to be closed off and stick to the familiar. Thus, an athlete who is open and flexible will continue to learn and improve. Similarly, coaches with high levels of Openness allow their athletes to experiment with different ways of training and competing, rather than trying to cram everyone into the same box.

Flexibility has also been identified as a key component of intelligence. According to the triarchic theory of intelligence proposed by psychologist Robert Sternberg in 1985, one of the three essential ingredients of intelligence is "practical intelligence" (the other two are "analytical" and "creative"). According to Sternberg, people with high practical intelligence can function well in their environments by adapting to their situation, selecting an environment that fits you better, or actively changing your environment to better suit your abilities. In all cases, it's essential to know and understand your environment to be effective in it. This requires openness and flexibility. Your race strategy for a flat, paved course on a cool day with low humidity will differ from your approach on a hot and humid day on rugged terrain.

If you find yourself resisting change or closed off to another way of doing things, ask yourself, "What am I afraid of?" Fear is often the reason we hold tight to the familiar. You may be afraid of failing at the new way, and that is in fact likely to happen at first, but you can overcome it with practice, as we will see in the next chapter. Or you could be afraid that the new way will be better than your old way, and then you would have to admit you were wrong, or at least that your old way wasn't the only way to be right. Yet to improve is to evolve, and to do that you need to be open to change.

There are very few areas in which there is only one way to succeed, and very few champions who have not evolved and changed along the way. We know of only one principle to which everyone must always adhere to achieve greatness, and that is the principle of deliberate practice. We'll talk more about that in Chapter 4.

How Champions Become Champions

"I wouldn't call Musashi ordinary. But he is. That's what's extraordinary about him. He's not content with relying on whatever natural gifts he may have. Knowing he's ordinary, he's always trying to improve himself. No one appreciates the agonizing effort he's had to make. Now that his years of training have yielded such spectacular results, everybody's talking about his 'god-given talent.' That's how men who don't try very hard comfort themselves."

—Japanese novelist Eiji Yoshikawa, *Musashi*

Raymond Berry, the Hall of Fame wide receiver and former 20th-round draft pick of the Baltimore Colts in 1954, is what we would call a self-determined athlete.

As described by Mark Bowden in his 2008 book *The Best Game Ever*, during his childhood, Berry would select a professional football game every week and watch film of it. Then he would choose a wide receiver and reconstruct the routes he ran on every play, whether or not he had been thrown the ball. Think about that last line: *whether or not he had been thrown the ball.*

Berry would, essentially, replay that model player's game on a vacant field, with nobody watching or advising him. He was a winner who toiled in isolation in pursuit of greatness.

This is deliberate practice.

Martin and Valent Sinković are two-time Olympic champions, world-record holders, and multiple-time world champions in various rowing disciplines. When asked about the keys to their success, they attribute it definitively to their training habits. "It's important to train hard and enjoy yourself," Martin says. Valent adds that consistency is crucial. "It's not just training for one big day and then taking a week off, or training for one or two weeks before the race, but consistently all year long."

In fact, the Sinković brothers train at least once a day (and usually twice) 362 days of the year, taking off only Christmas, New Year's Day, and Easter. "Everything you do in training is measured by the race," Valent says. "The race is a reflection of everything you do in the whole year." The brothers also credit their coach, Nikola Bralic, for teaching them much of their training mentality. They both note how he provides a specific goal and rationale for each training session.

This is deliberate practice.

Up to this point, we have emphasized that there is more than one way to be a champion and that champions learn and grow and contradict themselves along their journey to success. For every rule, there is an exception, and for every valuable trait, there is a point at which it becomes detrimental. Now we have arrived at a meta-exception—a guiding principle for which there is no exception and a trait that cannot become too extreme. That principle (and that trait) is deliberate practice.

This type of training is essential to success, and no validated theory or proper study has shown that we can train too hard or practice too much. Rather, the benefits of deliberate practice never cease. Sure, you can cause damage or setbacks if you train in a tough-stupid manner, but the evidence is clear that those who put in a sustained effort to improve continuously over time are the ones who become great. There are undoubtedly some who work their butts off and don't become world champions, but everyone who reaches that championship level has put in the work.

Yet people who are strangers to excellence often assume that champions have some genetic "God-given" advantage over others that allows them to reach those great heights. This is a tempting proposition when watching someone else do things we wish we could do; telling ourselves that they are simply blessed with good genes is a way of saving face. If we attributed their success to their work ethic instead, we would have to face the question of whether we're willing to do that kind of work ourselves. Instead, we let ourselves off the hook and declare: "I could never do that," "What I'd give to have his genes!" and "You just can't teach that kind of feel for the game."

In reality, these statements show a lack of respect for the hard work the elite competitor has put in. They also let the spectator feel less at fault for their own mediocrity. They can sit back and believe that there is nothing they can do about it. But there actually is something they can do: they can get out there and train.

Nurture over Nature

When it comes to the nature vs. nurture argument, the research and science, if not public opinion, favor nurture in driving the development of expertise. In other words, the determining factors in achievement and success have far more to do with our habits and hard work than our natural ability. Although genetics and natural talents may play a role in some disciplines (this is an ongoing debate among scientists and researchers), their influence can be overcome through experience and deliberate practice. This holds

look pass or "magically" anticipates their opponent's movements. While we can marvel at their "feel for the game," this feel was not something they were born with but rather something they developed over many years of intensive practice.

The expert may need only two or three pieces of information to figure out the entire pattern, through a process known as "chunking." They have seen these patterns hundreds or even thousands of times in practice and competition, and they became a bit more efficient each time. We see this skill demonstrated by great athletes and other experts as well, including the referee who always seems to be in the perfect position to make a call, the waiter who gets everyone's order right without having to write it down, and the veteran teacher who separates kids in their classroom as they complain, "But I haven't done anything!" True, they hadn't acted out *yet*, but the teacher saw the pattern, as they'd seen it a thousand times before, and acted in anticipation of what was about to happen.

These examples of pattern recognition and accurate anticipation and response all reflect a level of expert performance. After many hours of training, tasks that used to require a high degree of attention and effort become more automatic. (See Chapter 10 for a more detailed discussion of moving from conscious to unconscious control.) The highly trained athlete appears to perform effortlessly. In reality, they trained for thousands of hours and did the hard work while you weren't watching to make things look so easy.

Making Your Practice Deliberate

Although there is no magic number of hours to become an expert in your chosen domain, those who become world-class in anything typically put in at least 10 years and 10,000 hours of deliberate practice before achieving that status. Much of what we know about this topic is owed to psychologist Anders Ericsson and his colleagues.

Ericsson, who was mentored by Herb Simon early in his career, observed experts ranging from musicians, athletes, and doctors to typists and waiters. His resulting theory of deliberate practice states that expertise requires more than simply putting in the time. It's not just the hours, but also what you do with those hours. Think of an activity you've done your entire life and still perform like a rookie, such as washing dishes. You might wash dishes several times a day, every day, yet still it takes you just as long as it always has. You're going through the motions and not getting better. We can also look at professional vs. recreational golfers. Some players golf for decades and never improve their scores, while a professional continually improves. Why is that? The answer is that the former is participating, but the latter is engaged in deliberate practice.

For practice to be deliberate, it must involve these three things:

1. Training with a particular goal in mind
2. Doing things that are not always fun
3. Receiving timely and accurate feedback

Let's take a closer look at these characteristics.

Training with a particular goal in mind: Let's say you meet two people on their way to a mandatory team practice, and you ask them what they plan to work on today. The person on a course toward mediocrity will tell you, "I don't know," or say, "I'll have to see what our coach has in mind." The teammate working toward expertise, in contrast, will have an answer at the ready. They might tell you they need to work on defending attacks to their left side, or finishing a match once they've gotten ahead, or camouflaging their attacks better, or counterattacking more consistently. The possibilities are endless, but the consistent factor is that the experts are invested in their own continuous improvement. To them, practice is not something you simply try to get through. It's an essential and valued opportunity to get better.

The first step is to acknowledge your imperfections. It's critical to have a mindset in which you see yourself as flawed. If you have a fragile ego or are afraid to acknowledge your weaknesses, you'll prevent yourself from improving on them. If you harbor deep levels of self-doubt, staring at your current shortcomings might make you believe that you don't have what it takes to be a winner, so you either deliberately or unconsciously become blind to your weaknesses. Another part of the winner's paradox, then, is that confidence allows you to own your flaws. Confidence begets humility and a recognition, no matter how good you are, that you have a lot to learn. And knowing that you're a long way from perfect doesn't make you feel ashamed—it makes you excited, because you get to continue your pursuit of excellence and keep improving as you go.

You could call this the "beginner's mindset," which you maintain even when you're an expert. Since a defining quality of an expert is to continually seek improvement, they are always open to learning and never think they know it all. If you're studying for a test, study the material you don't know as well. If you're afraid you might fail, you may be tempted to avoid the topics that cause you trouble, but that just makes your fears more likely to become reality. If you have a learner's mentality, you'll gravitate toward those topics. Every time you face something you don't know and learn something new, you increase your chance of success.

When you're highly confident, finding a weakness isn't scary. It's a golden opportunity to get better, and that's why you're practicing in the first place. Picture eating an ice cream cone on a hot day. If you've done this, you know that the ice cream starts to melt and drip down over the cone, and you have to lick the melted part first before it drips all over your hand and makes a mess. In this metaphor, the dripping part is your biggest weakness, and licking it symbolizes deliberate practice. You're constantly circling the cone to find and fix your weaknesses and turn them into strengths. It's a cyclical process where you keep improving all aspects of your game, and the process never ends until your ice cream is all gone and you've reached your retirement. At that point you can decide on a new endeavor and direct your efforts there.

Doing things that are not always fun: Deliberate practice is often exhausting and painful. Fighters targeting their weaknesses are sparring in positions and with techniques that they're currently lacking, and they get beat up—at least in the short term. Figure skaters are working on jumps and other techniques they haven't yet mastered, and they fall frequently. Deliberate practice can quite literally hurt, and experts must have the resilience and grit to persevere through a years-long difficult grind. This requires you to delay gratification and stay motivated when the reward for all your hard work is much farther down the road. To persevere, you have to want to do it. Psychologists would say you need a sense of self-determination, and that's hard to find when someone else is forcing you to do something. (More on this in a moment.)

Receiving accurate and timely feedback: Logically, in order to improve, you need a way to evaluate yourself. Without this, you are shooting blindly, and you could be working really hard without actually getting better. With certain skills, the feedback comes naturally and obviously. If you're an archer working to improve your aim, seeing where your arrow penetrates the target gives you solid information about how you're doing. The same goes for shooting a basketball—it's immediately clear whether you've shot it well or poorly. For other skills, getting feedback requires more support, typically in the form of a coach or a training partner.

Are you throwing that combination properly or sinking that submission in more perfectly today than you were yesterday? Although you may have a feeling about it, you need someone else to verify whether your feeling is correct. This means having good people around you who are willing to give you accurate feedback, both compliments and criticisms. And you need to be open to hearing it. If you want to improve, you need to have the mind of a learner, eager to know what you're doing right or wrong, well or poorly, to get better every day.

Keith Gavin, an NCAA wrestling champion and head wrestling coach at the University of Pittsburgh, emphasizes the importance of being analytical about what happens during practice. "Some guys want to leave practice and not even think about what happened," he says. "But it's important to do the analysis." He encourages his athletes to reflect after every practice on what they did well, what they did wrong, and how they're going to improve.

Having a coach and teammates who promote your growth in this way is invaluable, but becoming a champion also requires self-motivation. Although it helps to have others encourage you, to sustain the effort over many years, the drive needs to come from within. That leads us to another important difference between experts and everyone else: experts spend more time practicing on their own.

This can make it more challenging to get feedback, but champions find a way. For example, young chess players with the internal drive to improve spend many hours practicing alone by using published records of games played by the masters. They look at these recorded games one move at a time and decide what they think the best next move would be. Then they turn the page to see how the chess master actually moved. That's their feedback. If the young player's choice matches it, they go on to the next move. If it doesn't, they pause and reflect until they see why the master's move was superior. Move by move and page by page, they learn and improve.

Being Self-Determined

Ask any winner, and you'll find they have spent an enormous amount of time working on their own to improve, over and above what was required by the official practice schedule. And just to clarify, hitting up a friend or teammate for an extra sparring session counts, even though there is another person there. The key is having the internal motivation to get it done. Doing something without having to be told—without the threat of getting in trouble or the prospect of being praised—shows self-determination. Self-determined individuals practice because they want to, not because they have to, even when it's not fun.

Given the importance of self-determination in pursuing excellence, a word is in order regarding the temptation we might feel to push someone toward deliberate practice. This temptation is especially strong when a young person demonstrates some talent or "natural ability" in a sport or other performance domain. Seeing a kid's potential and knowing the importance of hard work to realize it, coaches and parents may try to teach a child about this and encourage them to make their best effort at all times. This makes some degree of sense, but ultimately that motivation will have to come from within if they're going to succeed over the long term.

When we look at experts' own histories, we find that their developmental process included a point where they *decided* they wanted to become great in their chosen domain. The vast majority of them didn't set out with that goal in mind. In fact, despite the common belief that you need to get kids started early so they don't fall behind, most champions discover what they want to pursue in earnest later in the process.

A seminal 1985 book by Benjamin Bloom called *Developing Talent in Young People* revealed that experts progress through a series of stages on their way to excellence. Bloom's subjects included athletes, musicians, mathematicians, and scientists. His research showed that, rather than deciding at an early age to pursue greatness in a specific domain (or having this decided for them by their parents), those who accomplish great things typically come to this pursuit over time.

Since then, other researchers, including Jean Côté and his colleagues, have built upon Bloom's work. Côté described a three-stage process he labeled the sampling, specialization, and investment years. In the first stage, young people try out or *sample* a variety of activities before eventually deciding to *specialize* in one of them. They later decide to *invest* in their chosen activity and pursue excellence in it. These findings support those of physiologists and physicians, who warn against the dangers of early specialization due to the risk of overuse injuries among children, whose bodies are still growing and maturing. In the end, though years of deliberate practice are required to achieve excellence, nobody but the future champions themselves can decide they want to pursue it. Parents and coaches can provide a supportive environment, of course, but the decision rests with the individual.

As we mentioned earlier, there is no upper limit to the benefit of deliberate practice, but you need to keep in mind that there *is* a limit to how much you can push yourself on a daily basis. The goal might be 10,000 hours or more of deliberate practice, but you cannot accrue them all in one day or one week.

Remember the tough-smart mantra—you should aim to push your mind and body to their brink but not beyond their breaking point. Even as we advocate for an extremist approach in the long term, we recognize the need for moderation in the short term. Just as a long-distance runner would be foolish to go all-out in the first 500 meters of a 10-kilometer run, as this leads to exhaustion and a slower overall time, any would-be champion should consider the big picture when deciding how hard to push yourself. A tough-stupid training mentality can lead to exhaustion and overuse injuries. Being tough-smart allows us to persevere across decades. When you consider the ballpark figure of 10 years and 10,000 hours to develop expertise, this averages out to 1,000 hours per year and approximately 20 hours per week of deliberate practice, or half the typical 40-hour workweek for a full-time employee.

All winners put in the work. This is the one hard fact you must recognize if you want to excel. Beyond their commitment to deliberate practice, though, there is very little all winners have in common.

Some would-be influencers may tell you that in order to excel you need to act and think a certain way. Unless they're telling you that you need to work hard and practice deliberately, take such advice with a grain of salt. They're giving you one way that works for some people. The idea of a "champion personality" was debunked decades ago. There are all kinds of personalities among world-class performers—they can be low-key or amped-up, serious or playful, egotistical or humble.

So long as you engage in deliberate practice—lots of it—you can be your unique self as you follow your own path toward greatness.

The False Dichotomies: "And" Over "Or"

CHAPTER 5

Caring Deeply AND Keeping It in Perspective

Caring Deeply	Keeping It in Perspective
Pros	**Pros**
• Promotes effort and commitment • Adds meaning to the struggle • Prevents us from having an "out"	• Reduces anxiety • Leads to humility • Promotes a balanced identity
Cons	**Cons**
• Can increase anxiety • Leads to an "emotional roller coaster" • Interferes with a balanced identity	• Can lead to giving yourself an "out" • Rationalizes lack of effort • Can lead to distractions
When to Use This Attitude	**When to Use This Attitude**
• When motivation is waning • When high effort and focus are needed • If you perform well under pressure	• To counter performance anxiety • When dealing with non-sport issues • When obsessiveness interferes with living your life

Caring Deeply AND Keeping It in Perspective: Pros, Cons, and When to Use

"Win with humility. Lose with dignity. But, damn it, don't lose!"

—Bob Siddens, West Waterloo [Iowa] High School wrestling coach

"When you're riding, only the race in which you're riding is important."

—Bill Shoemaker, Hall of Fame jockey

To be a champion, you have to subscribe to every sports cliché there is. Go all-in. Give 110 percent. Live and breathe your sport. Spend practice time, free time, and even sleep time thinking about how to improve.

Why? Because winning feels great, and losing feels like your soul got run over by a tank. Knowing how important their sport is to themselves and those around them, champions act accordingly, working hard and making wise choices about diet, sleep, and lifestyle.

Still, some of these same champions, who devote their lives to their sports, know that it is not the entirety of life. We've all heard the clichés: Keep it in perspective. Remember there are more important things in life. Maintain a healthy work-life balance (or sport-life balance, in this case). Despite their devotion to their craft and the weighty expectations of their supporters, they place value on things beyond winning, such as abiding by the rules and maintaining a sense of humility. This does not diminish their commitment, though. They care just as deeply while knowing that sport is a part of life, not life itself.

For some competitors, the more they care, the more nervous they feel. These are the athletes who dominate in the practice room and excel in sparring but somehow can't rise to the occasion during a match. Since this type of athlete experiences performance anxiety and tends to "choke" under pressure, some coaches and psychologists help them by framing even the big competitions as low-stakes events. If you perform at your best under low or moderate pressure, you can use various methods and tricks to keep the perceived pressure low in your mind, both before the event to calm your nerves and, if necessary, after it to soothe the pain of a loss.

Most strategies for evading the sense of high stakes ahead of the competition involve maintaining a "healthy perspective" about the event, such as reminding yourself that it's not life or death and that your mother will still love you whether you win or lose. (Hopefully!)

If by coincidence a competitor has a loved one who dies or who is gravely ill around the time of an important contest, then this can serve as a real-life reminder that the sport is not everything. With this perspective, the anxiety-prone athlete feels less pressure and is, therefore, less likely to choke under it.

Interestingly, a similar psychological dynamic can happen when you've had a mild injury, but are still able to compete. The injury gives you mental "cover": if you perform poorly, you and everyone else can attribute your poor performance to your injured status, which is a factor beyond your control. You will seem courageous for even attempting to compete while in pain. At the same time, if you win, you're a hero for pulling out a victory against overwhelming odds. Competing with an injury lowers the stakes—no one blames you if you lose, and you get extra admiration if you win.

After a competition, if you've lost and feel terrible about it, try to ease your pain by reminding yourself that you have people who love you, this is not what defines you as a person, and nobody died. However, there is a long-term risk to this strategy because you are making losing more tolerable. Entering a future competition with the mindset that it's OK to lose will not bode well for you, especially when you're up against an opponent for whom losing is not an option.

Legendary New York Yankee Derek Jeter—as described by Tom Verducci in his 2009 *Sports Illustrated* article about that year's SI Sportsman of the Year—"jumped all over" a teammate who had performed poorly in a 2001 World Series loss after his teammate said, "Well, at least I had fun."

According to Verducci's article, when recounting that moment years later, Jeter said, getting upset all over again, "Fun? I can't relate to it . . . What makes me angry is when people don't care— not when they fail; everybody fails—or when people act like they don't care."

University of North Carolina head wrestling coach Rob Koll, a former NCAA champion for UNC and consistent winner as the head coach at Cornell and then Stanford, describes his "unfaltering, almost pathological" hatred of defeat. "This drives and motivates me like nothing else," Koll says. "This doesn't mean you have to act like a child if you lose, but it does need to drive you. After we lose a dual meet or recruit, I work twice as hard."

Rob goes so far as to suggest there's an evolutionary component operating here. "I think this is a much more honest and primal assessment of motivation," he says. "As our Neanderthal brethren evolved, defeat equated to death. Victory was certainly important but perhaps not as directly associated with survival."

Caring this deeply means that success feels exhilarating, and failure is life-or-death dreadful. If you allow yourself to experience the awful horror that comes with dedicating yourself to the singular pursuit of a goal and then failing to reach it, the pain of that disappointment might help you find even more energy and resilience so that you won't be disappointed next time.

Ask anyone who has achieved their ultimate goal, and they will tell you that part of their journey included painful setbacks that inspired them to find another level of commitment. Legendary wrestler and coach Dan Gable was undefeated through high school and college before being upset in his last match by Larry Owings in the 1970 NCAA finals. Gable has said that as successful as he was up to that point, he needed that loss to revitalize his commitment and eliminate any sense of invincibility. It was after this loss, he says, when "I got good." He then set his sights on an Olympic gold medal, which he earned in 1972 without giving up a single point.

Stories such as these show that great accomplishments can be heavily fueled by the pain of losing. Rather than trying to maintain perspective and soften the blow of their latest failures, champions channel that pain into greater effort and resolve. In this regard, attempting to convince yourself that "it's just a game" is missing the point. Instead of mentally reducing the stakes, find a way to rise up and perform your best when the stakes are high so you can avoid that awful disappointment in the future.

Consider a situation where your performance is literally a matter of life and death. Such scenarios occur regularly for surgeons, pilots, and military leaders, and for them, there is no escaping the pressure. If you're guiding a group of soldiers on a mission through hostile territory, then maintaining perspective means being aware that others' lives are in your hands. You must be at your best when it matters most.

Obviously, not everyone is cut out for this type of job. If you falter under high pressure, you should choose another career path. In military combat, emergency medicine, and law enforcement, you don't have the luxury of modifying the stakes to your preferred stress level. Rather, you must adapt your performance to the high-stakes reality. For those who can do this successfully, the stress of a sport competition pales in comparison. It should be no surprise, then, that athletes who have experienced challenging circumstances in their lives—such as a combat tour or growing up in a crime-ridden neighborhood or a war zone—often are the most resilient and mentally tough competitors.

Until you've experienced the kind of life-or-death pressure we're talking about, it's impossible to know how you'll respond. Psychologists refer to this natural reaction as your dominant response, and the way to determine your dominant response to stress is to put yourself in a stressful situation and see how you perform. Just as physical strain will reveal flaws in the integrity of a structure, highly stressful situations will expose our deepest psychological vulnerabilities—or highlight our greatest strengths.

Is your dominant response to stress to buckle down and focus on the task at hand? Or do you respond by freezing up and hoping you'll survive? If it's the former, then bring on your toughest opponents and fight like your life is on the line. But if it's the latter, keep your perspective and treat your sport like a sport, not a war. In the meantime, work on your dominant response so you can rise up to bigger challenges in the future.

Training to Thrive Under Pressure

How do you learn to be cool under pressure? This is a core instinct—you can't just tell yourself to have a different visceral response. How, then, can you make it instinctual to be a fierce competitor?

The answer, as always, is to train: to practice in a manner that prepares you for competition. This skill cannot be accomplished merely by drilling your techniques, however; it requires simulating the pressures of competition. Of course, the more high-stakes competitions you experience, the more opportunities you have to learn how to deal with the pressure. If you panic the first time you're under the spotlight, you'll know that going into the next competition and be able to adapt. This is why many coaches arrange for their athletes to face difficult challenges early in a season, so they're battle-tested by the time the championship tournaments come around.

Though it may be impossible to perfectly replicate the stress of competition in the gym or practice room, there are ways to approximate it. A common example is a coach setting up a sparring situation in practice where the loser must do push-ups or some other physical exercise, as a way to raise the stakes slightly. A step up from there would be to make the whole team do push-ups or wind sprints if the target athlete loses a round. In Spartan Races, competitors who fail to complete an obstacle face an increasing number of burpees in order to complete the course. Feel the pain of failure enough, and you learn to get it right.

We discussed the concept of deliberate practice in Chapter 4, and one of its defining aspects is going into it with a goal in mind—including goals related to building resilience under pressure. If you kick butt in practice and falter in competition, then you, along with your coaches, need to make the experience of practice more like competition (as an alternative to making competition more like practice in your mind). Some coaches broadcast crowd noise into their practices and hire hecklers to harass their athletes.

We know of a football coach who simulated the pressure of kicking a game-winning field goal by having the entire team watch the placekicker attempt a 50-yarder at the very end of each practice. If he made it, practice was over. If he missed it, everyone had to do a 12-minute run. That's a lot of pressure on the kicker each day, which is a great way to prepare for executing when the game is on the line.

Some fight gyms like to go hard in sparring so the fighters can get used to the actual stress of getting hit or even breaking a bone. If you're getting into real fights every day in the gym, then fighting an opponent in a competition won't be that big of a leap. Of course, this raises the risk of injury during training, so there is some trade-off in practicing under fight-time conditions.

The point is that your ability to perform well under pressure is something you can control. You can train your mind through deliberate practice, just as you can train your body for strength and endurance. It's not easy, but if it were, everyone would do it.

And this brings up another option, which is to avoid stressful situations altogether. Choosing a low-stress job does not make you a lesser person. You can live a happy and productive life without facing your fears every day. But if you tend to choke under pressure and want to change, there are options for you.

Sometimes an individual's relationship to pressure is formed at an early age, as when a kid is pushed into competition by their parents, who berate or shame the child for losing. If you're 6 years old when this happens, you might start associating competition with being yelled at and feeling like a bad kid who has disappointed your parents. You work hard, get older, and build some skills, but high-pressure situations still make you feel like a 6-year-old about to get in trouble, and all you want is a place to hide. If this is the case, training to get used to the pressure might make a small dent, but it's like putting a Band-Aid on a bullet hole.

Dominique Moceanu, who became the youngest gymnast to win the all-around title at the U.S. National Championships (at age 13 in 1995) and the youngest to win an Olympic gold medal (at age 14 in 1996), knows the risks of both coaches and parents losing perspective and putting too much pressure on a child. Now a successful coach and owner of the Dominique Moceanu Gymnastics Center, she describes the importance of loving a child unconditionally, without regard to performance. Recounting her experience winning Olympic gold as a team member, after falling in her individual vault, Dominique recalls feeling "completely disregarded as a person by my coaches and my father for not performing perfectly enough to suit them," even as she was receiving her medal. Describing the effect this had on her, she says, "I was so distraught and so sad. I was crushed, and it deeply scarred me." Her takeaway from this experience is clear: "You cannot make your love for your children based on the outcome—ever. It needs to be unconditional."

For someone who carries scars like these, addressing this problem might require one-on-one work with a sport psychologist or therapist. If you think that seeing a therapist is shameful, consider how you might handle a physical injury. If you're hurt and want to overcome your injury, then you'll see a doctor, get the surgery, and do the physical therapy to return to form. The same holds true for a psychological injury. If you want to get better, then you'll see a therapist and do the work, including being honest with yourself.

Matching Your Approach with Your Mental Skills

Let's accept that not everyone exudes grace under pressure—so how do you approach high-pressure situations while you're trying to improve? What do you do if you're an athlete who kicks butt when the stakes are low, but falters when they're high?

Let's consider the analogous physical or technical situation. How would you approach a fight with a physically or technically superior opponent? It would be foolish to pretend you can do things you can't. Though belief in yourself is important, it's equally important to have an accurate assessment of your abilities. If you're an excellent grappler and a novice striker in an MMA fight against a seasoned kickboxer, it would be foolish to stand and trade. Your best bet is to get the fight to the ground, even as you're training every day to improve your striking. You compete based on your present skill set while you continually work to improve.

The same goes for your mental skills: compete with the mindset that's best suited to your current psychological makeup while working to improve your mental game. You may recall from Chapter 3 that *practical intelligence* is the ability to function effectively in an environment, and there are several ways to do so. When the environment is a competitive, high-pressure one, you can adapt to it. (Admittedly easier said than done.) Another option is to alter the environment itself to better suit your skills. If you can change how you perceive the competitive environment, you effectively become more practically intelligent.

If you're at your best when viewing sport as nothing more than a game, lean into that mindset even if you're in the finals of a major tournament or fighting for a title. You can use self-talk of the type described earlier in this chapter to remind yourself what *isn't* at stake, that this is a competition and not a litmus test for your value as a person, and that it's a sport that's supposed to be fun. Base your approach on what works for you—embracing pressure may work in one situation, and keeping it in perspective may work in another.

You can also go with both approaches at the same time. People are walking contradictions. We frequently approach challenges with both excitement and fear, experience joy and sadness together, and have love-hate relationships with other people and things.

It should be no surprise, then, that we can both care and not care at the same time, and a setting where this happens every day is in play. As George Sheehan, a physician and philosopher of running, wrote in a 1975 *New York Times* piece, "In play you realize simultaneously the supreme importance and the utter insignificance of what you are doing. And you accept the paradox of pursuing what is at once essential and inconsequential."

If you've ever battled it out with a teammate until you're both beyond exhaustion, with nothing on the line beyond your internal drive, you know what Sheehan is describing, and you can bring the same attitude to competition. Sheehan added, "Violence and dissent are part of its joy. Territory is defended with every ounce of our strength and determination, and moments later we are embracing our opponents and delighting in the game that took place." If you welcome this concept of play, you need not decide whether to care deeply or keep it in perspective. You can do both.

Focusing on the Task at Hand

What exactly happens when someone chokes under pressure? What is going on in their head? Although people's answers vary, they fall into two major categories: emotional (what you feel) and cognitive (what you think).

Emotional: People who falter under pressure typically have high levels of anxiety. They respond to high stakes by feeling scared, and when you're frightened, it's hard to perform at your best—especially when making decisions. As we discussed in Chapter 2, there is an inverse relationship between your arousal level and the amount of information you can process. The more anxious you are, the slower and more error-prone your decisions become. To combat this, you can use techniques to reduce anxiety, such as controlled breathing and meditation. If the anxiety is deep-seated, however, these interventions typically have limited impact, and you will need to take a more in-depth look at your emotional response to pressure.

Cognitive: Generally the issue here is thinking about the outcome, rather than the task at hand. When the stakes are high, there is greater incentive to think about the consequences of failure. But the greater the consequences, the more important it is to focus on the task itself. Attention is a limited quantity, and an expert directs it where it's needed the most. Lives depend on the performance of military personnel and first responders, who are aware of the responsibility they hold. But they are not thinking about the high-stakes outcomes when they're doing their jobs. They're paying attention to the task at hand: surgeons focus on cutting precisely, police officers in a "shoot or don't shoot" situation focus on a suspect's movements, elite fighters focus on their opponent's motion to decide when to close the distance.

Psychologists refer to this type of focus as *high task orientation*. When you are oriented toward the task, other considerations go to the back of your mind and you focus on the process of what you are doing rather than on the outcome. (We'll talk about this in greater detail in Chapter 6, including how and when to shift from one to the other.) In the midst of competition, all your mental energy is needed to focus on the task at hand. When you've learned how to do this effectively, the outcome will take care of itself.

Famed wrestler and coach Dan Gable emphasizes this point as well. "Focus on what you are doing," he says. "If you're wrestling, then focus on wrestling, not on how you feel." He recounts several instances of finishing a match and wondering, "How did I just do that? I can hardly walk," or "I can't believe how tired I am." He noticed these things only after the job was done. "When you're in the actual situation, focus on what needs to be accomplished," Dan explains. "When your mind starts meandering, that's when you get into trouble. You need to focus on finishing strong."

Martin and Valent Sinković, the champion rowers, also strive to focus on the task rather than the outcome or any pressure associated with high expectations. "Since winning our first world championship in 2010, we have been the favorites in every race," Valent says. "Instead of thinking about that, we go into each race and focus on doing our best that day."

Keith Gavin, the NCAA wrestling champion and University of Pittsburgh coach, describes a similar challenge during his time as a competitive wrestler. An underdog through much of his college career, Keith says he was unburdened by expectations. But when he won a national championship, he became aware of what he was "supposed to" achieve. "Sometimes when you get to a certain level," he says, "that expectation becomes an obstacle to just doing what you love to do."

The challenge is not to let your success contaminate the mindset that got you there in the first place. We'll explore this challenge further in the next chapter when we discuss intrinsic and extrinsic motivation.

Caring Deeply and Living in the Real World

Even for those who have dedicated their lives to their sport and tied their joy or heartbreak to their latest win or loss, there's still reason to maintain perspective. If you forget that sport is not the entire world, you will have trouble functioning in this larger reality. Your victory may place you above your opponents on the podium, but it does not place you above the law or excuse you from your responsibilities as a citizen.

The most admirable winners exhibit a level of humility that often surprises their fans and fellow competitors. Having accomplished great things in their craft, they feel no need to act superior. They're proud of themselves and don't need to brag or belittle anyone else.

Keeping things in perspective also means valuing sportsmanship and decency. As much as you might hurt after a loss, suck it up and shake your opponent's hand. If you need to throw a tantrum, find somewhere to do it in privacy. Remember that you're building a reputation not only as an athlete, but also as an individual and a representative of those who support you. And although you may be a hero at the moment, your time as a superstar won't last forever. You should be proud of yourself, but you should also stay humble.

Now, some of you may have no problem with humility, and some may value it so much that it actually holds them back. We've worked with many competitors who are so opposed to thinking of themselves as better or more deserving than another person that it leads to a lack of confidence. Recall from Chapter 2 that when we highly value a certain characteristic, we may avoid any movement toward its opposite trait. To an extremely humble person, confidence may feel like arrogance. So too for highly empathetic people—they may lack the "killer instinct" because they care too much about their opponents.

For these people, by keeping their sport in perspective, they can give themselves permission to operate by a different set of values than the one they use in the real world. Whereas they might never act like they're superior in their social circle, in a sport setting they can adopt a mentality that they're so superior that nobody deserves to be in the ring with them. Though in real life they're considerate and care about other people's feelings, in sport they can view their opponent as an enemy who's trying to take what they've worked for and pummel them for it. Just as a shy and socially awkward person can blossom at a costume party, a humble and easygoing person can transform into a demon when the bell rings and return to their gracious self when the contest is over.

This willingness to use one set of values in the sport context and another set in real life is known as *game reasoning*, as described by David Shields and Brenda Bredemeier. According to this theory, you accept that when you're playing a game (or fighting a fight, as the case may be), the standards of conduct are vastly different than in the real world. You might never punch someone in the face in your daily life, yet it's perfectly acceptable in the cage. You're free to go all in on being a warrior in there. You don't have to choose between caring deeply and keeping it all in perspective. You can do both.

A healthy perspective about your sport or career also comes in handy when it's time to retire. In combat sports, this happens when you're still quite young, relatively speaking, and there is a lot of life left after you've hung up your gloves or left your shoes on the mat. If your sport has been the center of your life and you've paid no attention to anything else, you're apt to have an identity crisis when your career is over. You may hang on way past your prime because you don't know what else to do. Perhaps you'll stay involved as a coach or trainer, or you might discover a whole new arena in which to compete. Many former champions find their way into business and other forms of leadership, leveraging the traits developed in their sport.

Former pro football player Chase Coffman spoke to us about the relative importance of sport in his life. A first team All-American tight end for the University of Missouri and eight-year NFL veteran, Chase says, "You have to look at yourself and your priorities and what you desire. Of course you care about the wins and losses, but after I got married and had kids, I realized regardless of whether I 'make it' or not, my wife and kids will still love me."

It's helpful to keep in mind that there is life after sport, though research with elite athletes has shown that they often prefer success over life itself—or at least they say so on surveys. In multiple studies done by Gabe Mirkin in the 1970s and Robert Goldman in the 1980s and '90s, about half of the athletes queried said they would take a pill that could guarantee them an Olympic gold medal even if it meant they would die within a year—or a variation of the question.

Is it admirable or pathological to sacrifice your health and well-being for your sport? The answer is a personal one, so decide for yourself. Assuming you survive your playing days, life will go on, and having tunnel vision could make your retirement quite difficult. But all of us don't need to be "well-rounded" people during our sport careers. If you're a true Renaissance man or woman, your life transitions are likely to go smoothly, but we need not explore all of life's opportunities at once.

"Balance is a misnomer," says Bruce Babashan, a renowned professional boxing trainer and former high-level business executive (his own career trajectory thus exemplifying his philosophy). "You can't have balance while being a fanatic about your goals." Bruce refers to "seasons of a life," with your full commitment to sport as one season. "The goal is not balance all the time," Bruce advises. "It's balance over time."

Of course there is more to life than your sport, but there are times when nothing else matters. So keep things in perspective, and go all-in as well.

CHAPTER 6

Focusing on the Process AND Focusing on the Outcome

Focusing on the Process

Pros

- Brings attention to the most pressing concerns
- Tends to reduce anxiety
- Often leads to the desired outcome

Cons

- Can lead to unwise competition strategies
- Places style over results
- May not promote a competitive fire

When to Use This Attitude

- To counter high anxiety
- To encourage hard work and training
- Early in a season or career

Focusing on the Outcome

Pros

- Leads to wise competition strategies
- Is a results-driven approach
- Matches the reality of a zero-sum contest

Cons

- Can lead to high anxiety
- Ignores the path to get to the outcome
- Distracts from the task at hand

When to Use This Attitude

- During "short time" in competition
- When setting long-term goals
- To boost motivation

Focusing on the Process AND Focusing on the Outcome: Pros, Cons, and When to Use

"For when the One Great Scorer comes to mark against your name,
He writes—not that you won or lost—but how you played the Game."
—Sportswriter Grantland Rice, "Alumnus Football"

"Winning isn't everything. It's the only thing."
—Henry Russell "Red" Sanders, Vanderbilt University football coach

There's a reason people keep score in everything from elite sports to backyard badminton: Everyone wants to win. (And it doesn't hurt if the winner gets a big, fat check for the victory.)

But keeping score isn't just about the outcome; knowing the score during your competition helps you decide on strategy: whether to push the pace if you're behind or slow it down if you're ahead and don't need to take any big risks.

Yet as we touched upon in the previous chapter, focusing on the outcome distracts you from the task at hand. Every bit of attention you give to the outcome means that much less mental space you have for the process. If you focus on the process, the outcome tends to take care of itself. In addition, thinking of the outcome, especially in a high-stakes situation, can raise your anxiety and lead to choking under pressure.

Winners focus on both the outcome *and* the process.

This dual focus applies to both the preparation and competition phases. During our training, we need a reason to embrace the grind. To go through all the blood, sweat, and tears, most of us need a promised payoff, or at least a chance at it. It would be foolish to do a job with no paycheck. This presents a barrier for new athletes, as it usually takes some time to see results. Your coach will tell you to "trust the process" and the victories will come eventually, but when you've never tasted success, it's hard to stay motivated. But once you get that first win, it's so much sweeter knowing that you've soldiered through some losses and hardship to get there.

Nick Gallo, an NCAA wrestling champion, two-time All-American for Hofstra University, and longtime wrestling advocate as a businessman, says athletes spend more time down than up. Nick, a recipient of the National Wrestling Hall of Fame's Lifetime Achievement Award in 2000, says, "But I learned to appreciate it, especially when the end result feels almost unreal." Nick was what many would call a "late bloomer." Having never placed higher than fourth in his high school state tournament, he describes his eventual successes as inexplicable. "I wish I could package the feeling and give it to others," he says. "Remembering throughout the journey what this euphoria feels like always would motivate me through the tougher days."

That taste of glory makes it easier to stay motivated and helps us endure the process. But what if you don't achieve the outcome you hoped for? Does that mean your time and efforts were wasted?

After all, no matter how many people are pursuing the same title, only one can win it. Does that mean it was all worth it for the one champion, and a tragic waste for the rest? If it were only about the outcome, then the answer would be yes—there's one winner and a bunch of losers. But if you value the process as well, the effort is not wasted. It still provides a payoff, one that is captured eloquently in President Theodore Roosevelt's oft-quoted "Citizenship in a Republic" speech from 1910, in which he contrasts the "critic" with "the man who is actually in the arena." Roosevelt describes such a man as one "who at the best knows in the end the triumph of high achievement, and who at the worst, if he fails, at least fails while daring greatly, so that his place shall never be with those cold and timid souls who neither know victory nor defeat."

Megan Moulton-Levy, an elite athlete member of the U.S. Tennis Association (USTA) board of directors and the general manager of player development at the Junior Champions Tennis Center, also emphasizes the importance of the process. She explains, "What I ask my players to really focus on is the journey and the pursuit of becoming the best. That's where the joy should come from. That, to me, is the outcome."

Boxing coach Bruce Babashan is a strong advocate for having a robust belief in yourself, of not just wanting to win but also knowing that you can. This core belief emerges from "a stew of commitment" that involves a great deal of suffering. The unyielding commitment to a goal drives this, though "you don't suffer for the performance," he says. "You suffer for the mindset. There is magic in it." You are driven to win, but "when you lose and do your best, you can live with the outcome."

The paradox is that to benefit fully from the process, you need to tenaciously seek an outcome. You need to want something so badly that you're willing to suffer for it. Without the destination, there's no journey. And although the journey often becomes the most valuable part, most people don't take the hard road just because they enjoy a bumpy trip. There's a fundamental difference between going through the motions and doing the hard work with a purpose in mind.

Intrinsic and Extrinsic Motivation

When you do something simply because you enjoy it, you're *intrinsically* motivated. You're driven by your love for the activity or the pleasure you get from doing it. When you eat your favorite food, you're intrinsically motivated by the taste. Likewise, when you're doing something just for fun—when you're playing—this is intrinsic motivation. You don't need to talk yourself into doing it.

Keith Gavin often asks the college wrestlers he coaches why they do the sport. "The answer you want to hear is you do it because you love what you do," he says, adding that dropping your attachment to winning and losing makes it easier to focus on doing what you love. He says this intrinsic motivation helps athletes continue to improve. "You're going to keep evolving your skill set if you truly love what you do," Keith says. "When you try to win by any means necessary or only stick to what you've done in the past, you're not expressing your joy for the sport."

Dominique Moceanu describes how one of her gymnasts got caught in a negative cycle by caring too much about winning a college scholarship. "She felt so much pressure to do well that she stopped enjoying the competition," Dominique explains. She intervened by telling the young gymnast, "Trust yourself. Instead of putting excessive pressure on yourself, relinquish control and have fun."

This sentiment was expressed eloquently by the late, great Dave Schultz, an Olympic and world champion in freestyle wrestling. As quoted by the U.S. National Wrestling Hall of Fame, he said, "To me it's not a sacrifice. It's a choice. I'm not wrestling for any other reason than I want to wrestle. So I'm doing what I want to do." Without a doubt, a burning level of intrinsic motivation allows many elite performers to persist.

Sometimes you're intrinsically motivated to train. It's fun to do a sport you love, especially when you're well-rested and fully hydrated and you're having success. If you're a bit of a masochist, you might even enjoy the suffering you endure when pushing past exhaustion or cutting weight or getting beat up by a quicker sparring partner.

Sooner or later, though, there comes a time when it's not fun at all, when heading to training or sweating out a few more pounds when you're already dehydrated is the last thing you feel like doing. At these times, the process is something you tolerate rather than crave. This is when focusing on the outcome can become your saving grace. When you have no intrinsic motivation, you need an *extrinsic* reason to persevere. Whereas intrinsic motivation is doing something for its own sake, extrinsic motivation is doing it to get something you want. As with the other dualisms we've covered, we don't consider one form of motivation better than the other. They both have their benefits. Whatever drives you to do what you need to do is helpful.

When you need that extra push to keep grinding, you can focus on the outcome. Reminding yourself that there's a competition coming up that you plan to win can give you the motivation you need even when it's no fun at all. The process has extrinsic value because it gets you closer to the outcome you want.

Coach Moceanu explains, "The hard work has to be done at the gym, leading up to the competition. That's where you care deeply—in the practices. That's where you're setting yourself up for the best chance to succeed. When you get to the competition, the work is done." As an experienced coach and competitor, she knows that although scores are awarded at competition, these outcomes are largely determined by the process leading up to it.

The process also has value in its own right, and that's where the intrinsic motivation comes in. Sometimes it's simply fun. When it's not, it still gives us the "magical" experience of suffering for a cause. It also makes the victories sweeter.

On a practical level, the journey keeps us in shape. When you're in training, you eat healthier, avoid harmful habits, and stay in top condition. In a combat sport, you're also more capable of defending yourself, and even if you never need to use your self-defense skills in real life, you walk around with a greater sense of confidence.

You also join a community of others who are striving for excellence. It is impossible to convey to someone what it's like to give yourself over to a dream. It's only fully understood by those doing the same. When you become part of this culture, it never leaves you, and that may be the most valuable part of the whole process.

The Process and Outcome in Competition

Up to this point, we've been describing the process-outcome duality as it pertains to training, but it is relevant to competition as well. Here, our considerations relate to our strategy and tactics. Which type of focus is more conducive to your best performance—or, more accurately, when is it best to focus on one or the other?

It depends.

It depends on the situation, as well as your own proclivities.

If you tend to get highly anxious and hampered by your nerves, you'll benefit from focusing more on the process during competition, since thinking about the outcome tends to raise anxiety levels. Rather than thinking about winning or losing, focus on a specific task. If you're looking to land your best strike, think about your timing and setting it up, but in the moment don't worry about getting the knockout. If you execute well, you'll get the result you want.

In contrast, if you think too much about the outcome, that's less attention you have to focus on what you need to do right now. If you're looking for the knockout, you'll be "loading up" on your shots and warning your opponent, which lets them easily evade you. Focusing too heavily on the outcome can impair your performance and prevent you from achieving it.

Now let's say you're behind on the scoreboard or on the judges' scorecards, and you need a finish to win. You need to be aware of this and respond accordingly. You might be tempted to tell yourself that you need a knockout (or a submission or a fall, as the case may be), and that's fine. If you're so skilled that your body knows how to make that happen, go ahead and focus on the outcome, and let your autonomic nervous system do the rest (see Chapter 10 for a more detailed discussion of our nervous systems).

But it's often not enough to think about the result without also focusing on your path to victory. Just as a coach would be remiss to tell you, "Knock them out" without offering any advice on tactics, your self-talk ought to guide you through the process. In the midst of competition, you have a microcosm of the destination and the journey, and it's helpful to focus on both.

Next let's assume you're on the opposite side of the previous scenario: You're way ahead of your opponent, and time is running short. How should you let the current scenario guide your actions? Should you play it safe by going on defense and cruising to victory, or should you push ahead and try to get the fall or the knockout, knowing that you have to take some risks to make it happen? Your answer depends on whether you prioritize just getting a win or *how* you win.

Consider the two quotes at the opening of this chapter. The first, penned by legendary sportswriter and Vanderbilt alumnus Grantland Rice, suggests that *how* you play the game ultimately determines your value. This sentiment appeals to athletes who are deeply committed to certain guiding principles, as well as to those who view themselves not only as competitors, but also as entertainers. Of the former, one example is someone committed to "always being the aggressor" or "never taking a backwards step." These athletes would rather "die on their sword" than follow an easy path to victory. Such approaches are entertaining for spectators, and many athletes value the entertainment aspect in and of itself. They want to be fun to watch, so they develop a style that makes them a fan favorite. To them, losing an exciting contest is more appealing than winning a boring one. The process takes precedence over the outcome.

Other athletes consider that foolish, and they have a point. The goal is getting the win—and the trophy or check that goes with it. To them, the notion that you're willing to set that aside to prove something to yourself (or the audience) seems ludicrous. It exemplifies a tough-stupid mentality, and one in which you're giving in to your ego rather than making smart decisions (more on this below). In contrast, if you adhere to Red Sanders' sentiment in the second quote, then the only thing that matters is winning, and you ought to do whatever you can to make that happen. Even if you personally believe in "moral victories," they don't get you to the next round of a tournament. Only an actual victory does. In the objective world of sport and combat, it's all about the outcome.

So which quote do you prefer? We could say that both are correct, depending on the circumstances. Yet regardless of where you stand on the process vs. outcome dichotomy, there are both big picture items and small details to consider.

Dream Big and Do the Little Things Each Day

Achieving greatness requires a vision, and that, in turn, requires thinking ahead to conceive of your future self as far more than you are right now. It also requires you to have faith so your daily setbacks and hardships don't distract you from your long-term goals. If your big dreams are to become reality, you must work to move yourself an inch closer to your goal each day and do that consistently over many weeks and years. When the grind becomes draining, it helps to focus on your greater dreams to remind yourself why you're doing all this hard work. You need to dream big and act daily.

In this framework, your dreams must focus on an outcome, since you're looking far down the road to where you want to be and who you want to become. Without this larger vision, or *purpose*, it's hard to stay motivated. When you wake up bruised and achy each morning with a long list of daily tasks to accomplish, you may ask yourself, "Why am I doing this?" If you don't have an answer, you'll either pull the covers back over your head or get up only half-committed to the day's requirements. We therefore recommend setting challenging long-term goals.

What are you planning to achieve over the next several years? Is it becoming a state champ? A world champ? Are you seeking a college scholarship? However successful you've been up to now, when setting your long-term goals, aim for more. Go big. Ask of yourself something that's beyond your current abilities. The goal should be challenging, yet something you believe is possible (not a fantasy). If you're still on the junior varsity team, it's a pipe dream to think you'll be a national champ by the end of the current season. But that could be your three-year goal or your five-year plan.

Dreaming big is a strong driver of momentous accomplishments, though it's only part of the equation. You also need to focus on the smaller, more short-term goals along the way. Whereas your long-term goals speak to the outcome, your short-term goals guide you through the process. So you want to be a state champ? That's an admirable goal that gets you out of bed each morning. The next question is: How are you going to make that happen? Your answer should be a roadmap composed of the little things you'll need to do on a daily basis. For every ambitious long-term goal, you need a series of short-term goals to pursue on the way.

These daily tasks include deliberate practice, of course, but also much more. They include being disciplined in your choices and actions. This means eating healthy food rather than junk, which sometimes requires you to prepare something yourself rather than consuming what they offer at the cafeteria. That in turn means you need to wake up earlier to make breakfast, which means you have to go to bed sooner to be well-rested. And *that* means saying no to some fun nights out. If you're in school, it also means paying attention in class and staying on top of your studying, so you don't have to cram for tests, which messes up your sleep schedule, or even worse, become academically ineligible.

It's easy to say you're planning to do great things. But what happens when the time comes to actually do them? Your daily actions show whether you really meant it when you declared your grand intentions.

"Everyone says they want to be a national champion, but what are you being faithful to right now?" asks Mark Ellis, the 2009 NCAA Division I heavyweight wrestling champion and a two-time All-American at the University of Missouri. He now inspires others to pursue their goals and passions, as the director of the Fellowship of Christian Athletes Wrestling Midwest . "Success to me now is completing what's right in front of me and then, once that is completed, putting the next thing right in front and focusing on that," he says.

Lots of people say they're going to achieve greatness, yet very few bring those statements to fruition. One obvious reason is that there's only one gold medal and many competitors, and it's a small fraction of competitors who even give themselves a shot at the gold. To put yourself in the mix, you need to believe you're capable of greatness, and there's a difference between voicing your dreams, believing in them, and acting on them with daily habits.

Chase Coffman, the University of Missouri All-American and NFL veteran, refers to a player's "body of work" in influencing the trajectory of their career, rather than one success or one mistake. He says that, with the help of a counselor from the NFL benefits program, he realized, "As long as you're consistently doing the right thing—like compound interest—day after day and week after week and month after month, these good habits are going to be more impactful than one or two mess-ups." In short, doing the right things each day is what counts the most.

We've been assuming here that your short-term goals are in service to your long-term goals—that is, you typically set the destination and then make the roadmap to get there. But you can look at it the other way as well and set long-term goals to galvanize your efforts each day.

When the hard work pays off and you achieve your major goals, you rarely pack it in and move on to other endeavors. Instead, you reset your goals in pursuit of even greater success. This pursuit gives greater meaning to each day. So long as you're motivated to improve continuously, the process goes on, and the so-called outcomes are merely points on the ongoing journey.

Paul McBeth, a six-time world champion in disc golf, says, "It's funny to say outcome, because it's something that never finishes. There's never a full outcome." It's a similar sentiment to the one voiced by legendary basketball coach John Wooden, who said, "Success is never final; failure is never fatal."

Play to Win and Not to Lose

The argument over whether you should play to win or play not to lose generates some passionate opinions on both sides. There are advantages to being the underdog—one of them is being able to play like there's nothing to lose. But when you're the favorite, you do have something to lose, and playing not to lose is widely considered an awful headspace to be in. The alternative is playing to win, which is endorsed by most psychologists and those power-of-positive-thinking folks. It's similar to the concept of influencing behavior through rewards rather than punishment. Punishment teaches you what *not* to do, while rewards teach you what *to* do. But many champions say they hate losing more than they love winning, and clearly it's led them to success time after time; punishment has been more effective than rewards in their case. The obvious conclusion is that you should play to win *and* not to lose.

We can't give you an exact recipe for your winning vs. losing strategy, but we can offer you some ideas to consider when formulating the best mindset for you and deciding when to lean in one direction or the other. Especially when it comes to playing not to lose, there is a great deal of emotional nuance in the ways people relate to losing.

For some competitors, the prospect of losing strikes them with fear. At worst, this fear is overwhelming, making it hard to think straight or function at all. They choke. For others, their aversion to losing is associated not so much with fear as with hatred. For example, as cited in the previous chapter, Rob Koll describes his "unfaltering hatred" of defeat. While fear of failure can lead to a "fight, flight, or freeze" response, hatred of it typically leads to a greater resolve to avoid it, helping you focus on what you need to do in the moment.

Based on this line of thinking, some coaches preach that their athletes should hate losing more than they love winning. Though this is an effective mindset for many, it doesn't fit everyone. Some competitors prefer to enjoy the process and focus on how wonderful it feels to win, rather than how awful it feels to lose. This tends to be a more peaceful existence (and you're easier to be around if you're exuding this kind of positive energy). If you can truly relish your successes, you'll have a more enjoyable experience overall. So go ahead and love winning. You can also hate losing and thus have motivation coming from both sides of the equation.

Analyzing your successes and failures can help you understand how you focus on winning or not losing. For instance, some athletes are "slow starters" and don't kick it into gear until their back is against the wall. Paul McBeth has never been deterred by a bad round or two. He learns from his mistakes and comes through reliably in the later rounds of a competition. This suggests that Paul and others like him are helped most by focusing on not losing, since they perform best when they're faced with the prospect of a loss. If this describes you, we suggest increasing your focus on "playing to win," which will help you push yourself from the start, rather than coasting until you need to step it up.

Ben's development as a wrestler reflects this as well. Though he had much success early in his career, it wasn't until late in college that he consistently competed with a strong level of urgency from the opening whistle. Though he had almost always come through in the end, once he set out to win from the get-go, Ben broke the NCAA record for most first-period pins.

Understand that being motivated not to lose isn't a bad thing. Indeed, if you don't hate losing, then if you fall behind or otherwise experience adversity, you might be tempted to just tank it and accept the loss. It's an advantage to be motivated not to lose—and it's even better when that's not your only motivation.

Other competitors have a difficult time closing out a match to secure the win. These are the fast starters and slow finishers who start out pursuing a win, but once they build a lead, they start worrying about blowing it and switch from being the hunter to the hunted. It's the same trap some people fall into when they're favored to win. In that unfortunate headspace, losing when you're "supposed to win" feels shameful.

In these scenarios, there are a few strategies for improving:

- Double down on your drive to win. Rather than let thoughts of losing creep in, stay focused not only on winning the bout, but on winning every minute and every exchange. The goal is to win and move on, and this ought to stay the same whether other people expect you to win or not.
- Work on your relationship to losing so that it is something you hate rather than something you fear. If you're favored to win, either based on your ranking going into the match or being in the lead halfway through, and you find your mind drifting to thoughts of losing, you want your self-

talk around it to be something like, "No way on earth am I letting them back into this match. Keep pouring it on." That's very different from, "Oh no, what if I blow this lead? That would be so embarrassing." The latter is fear-based and harmful, while the former is helpful.

- Don't think about winning or losing, but stay focused on the process, which is where this chapter began. Just as you change tactics throughout a competition depending on what is and isn't working, you'll benefit from developing multiple attitudes and ways to focus. We don't judge something as good or bad on principle, but rather on its impact. If it helps you, then it's the right thing to do.

Hate Losing and Seek Out Challenges

There's another paradox inherent among the most driven competitors, especially those who hate losing. The surest way to avoid a loss is to avoid competition altogether—or you could only compete against inferior opponents as a *sandbagger*: someone who downplays their skills to win a trophy, such as a purple belt entering a white belt division at a tournament. This approach is disdained by true competitors, of course. The champion's paradox, then, is that despite hating to lose, they pursue the strongest challengers rather than the easiest opponents.

When you have a winning record, you don't withdraw from competition to protect your perfect season; you set your sights on defeating tougher and tougher opponents. When you reach a new max in the weight room or overcome an obstacle that has stopped you in the past, you set your goal higher still. You hate to fail, but you continually put yourself in situations where failure is a real possibility. This means finding the toughest sparring partners, those who are strongest where you are weakest, so you can get better all the time.

If all you cared about was not losing, you would not challenge yourself. We aren't saying that those who claim to despise losing are lying—just that they despise cowardice even more. Champions and those with a champion's mentality are drawn to the toughest challenges like a magnet. They could easily get off the roller coaster ride that is a competitor's lifestyle—filled with alternating bouts of elation and heartache. But there's something about this road that attracts them. For some, it's the love of the sport, an intrinsic enjoyment of the task. For others, it's a desire to prove how good they can be, to build up their own egos and pride.

Task and Ego Orientation

The dual motivations to accomplish a task and boost your ego are analogous to a process and outcome focus, respectively. Originally developed by educational psychologists, goal orientation theory suggests that whenever you engage in an activity, you do so with a goal in mind. Further, these goals can be sorted into categories, such as task-oriented and ego-oriented goals.

As the term implies, when you're task-oriented, your main focus is to complete the job. If you're trying to hit a ball or a person, that's what you're thinking about. Having a strong task orientation correlates with being process focused.

When you're ego-oriented, you're aware of how good or how bad you are, even as you're doing whatever you're doing. You might be trying to prove your doubters wrong, so each time you score a point, you get some extra satisfaction from it. This can also help you muster that little something extra and elevate your game, because you want it more. In another, less helpful scenario, if you're the underdog in a competition and you're falling behind, your ego-oriented focus could have you questioning whether you're good enough to hang with your opponent. Alternatively, if you falter when you're favored to win and feel ashamed, it's because your ego is threatened. When your ego is at stake, the pressure is higher, which can bring out your best or make you choke, depending on how well you handle it.

An ego orientation can also be a problem in the practice room, where the focus should be on learning and improving. But if you're trying to prove that you're better than your training partners, you'll be less likely to experiment with a new technique or put yourself in positions where you're not skilled. This prevents you from improving on your weaknesses, and it stops your partners from learning as well. Don't be that guy. If you look at practice as just a way to show how good you are, you'll actually prevent yourself from getting better and annoy your teammates.

A highly ego-oriented approach also leads you to focus heavily on outcomes: the final score, the prize money, or the approval of your parents or coaches. This, as we've discussed, can be a problem. Since your attention is limited, devoting some of it to the outcome means you're giving less to the task, which often means your performance suffers. Coach Keith Gavin has observed that athletes are frequently hampered by these ego-oriented concerns. "They need to become aware of what's holding them back, and oftentimes, it's tied to ego," he explains.

In contrast, a task-oriented approach allows you to focus on the process. Rather than worrying about the result, you're free to focus on issues such as your technique, the "feel" of the action, and the joy of competing. There are some real advantages to this approach, and many coaches will tell you that if you stay focused on the process, the outcome will take care of itself. One reason is that a process focus tends to keep anxiety low. Think of a basketball player at the free throw line with two shots and one second left in the game. If they're worried about being responsible for winning or losing the game, the pressure could cause them to be unsteady and miss. But staying in a task-oriented, process-focused state would keep things simple, and it would be just another free throw.

For these reasons, many sport psychologists promote a task-orientated approach. But when deciding which approach is right for you, consider again how well you handle pressure. If you're the type of competitor who enjoys the spotlight and performs best when you're faced with being a "hero or a zero," an ego-oriented, outcome-focused approach could help you thrive. Another practical advantage to an outcome focus is especially apparent late in the game or fight, when you just need to score or prevent your opponent from scoring, whichever the case may be. If you're ahead on points with 30 seconds left, it would be foolish to take a big risk; instead, play it safe and secure the win. The idea of giving your all at all times is fine, but wins and losses have consequences, and pretending otherwise would be foolish.

Another difference between an ego-oriented and task-oriented approach is that in the former you compare yourself to others, while in the latter you judge yourself against your own past performance. In a task-oriented approach, the goal is to see self-improvement, regardless of where you stand among your competitors or even in comparison to your teammates. Since you can't control what others do, this is a healthy and generally risk-free way to evaluate your progress. Hats off to the youth sport coaches who tell their athletes not to worry about how good other people are, but to focus on improving their own performance.

Some sports lend themselves nicely to self-comparison, such as anything that's based on speed or distance. You ran a mile in 5 minutes flat last fall, and now in the spring you're running a 4:55. Excellent job. You're improving. But it gets harder when there's no objective gauge like the clock or the tape measure and the only way to evaluate your progress is to see how you stack up against the competition. In this case, even when you're task-oriented, you need to compare yourself to others; for example, how you're performing against your sparring partners. Your opposition becomes your personal yardstick. An important caveat, though, is that progress relative to your opponent doesn't necessarily mean beating them. It might mean coming closer to beating them than you did last time, or if you won last time, winning by a bigger margin.

One final warning about your ego orientation being too strong: If you're overly concerned about preserving your self-image or if your ego is too fragile, you may be incentivized to make less than a full effort. In other words, you may make up an excuse if you fail. You can tell yourself, "I didn't try my best, so my performance doesn't show how good I can really be." There's no need to engage in such mental gymnastics when you're focused on the task instead of the outcome. All that matters is getting the job done.

As with the other dichotomies we've addressed, when we look at the benefits of a task-oriented vs. ego-oriented mindset, it's not an either-or question. You just need to learn which one serves you better. Also, these are not opposite ends of a single spectrum, but two mindsets you always possess. Sometimes you're high in one and low in the other, and at other times you're high in both.

If you look back at Figure 1.1 on page 22 the second diagram captures this, where you can view task orientation as one arrow and ego orientation as the other. There is actually a test that can assess your level on each, called the Task and Ego Orientation in Sport Questionnaire (TEOSQ). Created by Joan Duda in 1989, this self-report assessment can give you an estimate of your default tendencies towards each orientation. In other words, you can measure the mindset that you adopt most of the time. This is not to imply that your tendencies dictate your goal orientations each moment. We all have predispositions, and it helps to know what they are. But you can alter your mindset to best adapt to the situation at hand.

Speaking of which, there is always room to adapt and improve. Each of us is a work in progress. But if you sometimes find yourself wondering if you'll ever be good enough, you're not alone. Read on to the next chapter to learn more.

CHAPTER 7

Thinking You're Good Enough AND Thinking You're Never Good Enough

Thinking You're Good Enough

Pros
- Produces high levels of confidence
- Encourages persistence through obstacles
- Provides an antidote to self-doubt

Cons
- Can lead to overconfidence
- Reduces motivation to improve
- Makes an athlete less coachable

When to Use This Attitude
- At competition time
- To counter moments of self-doubt
- When you're in awe of other competitors

Thinking You're Never Good Enough

Pros
- Promotes a mindset of continuous improvement
- Leads to being coachable
- Conveys a need for hard work

Cons
- Can lead to low confidence
- Reduces appropriate risk-taking
- On bad days, can be disillusioning

When to Use This Attitude
- At practice time
- To counter moments of low motivation
- When your ego has become too big

Thinking You're Good Enough AND Thinking You're Never Good Enough: Pros, Cons, and When to Use

"Evolve or die."

—Origin unknown

"I am the greatest. I said that even before I knew I was. I figured that if I said it enough, I would convince the world that I was really the greatest."

—Champion heavyweight boxer Muhammad Ali

"The curious paradox is that when I accept myself just as I am, then I can change."

—Psychologist Carl R. Rogers, *On Becoming a Person: A Therapist's View of Psychotherapy*

Your coach has been riding your butt all week: "Your footwork needs to get better." "You've got to improve your head movement." "What in the world are you doing with your hands?"

Even when you dominate in sparring and look to him for approval, he shakes his head and says you took your foot off the gas pedal too soon. Nothing pleases him.

But when you walk to the ring for the match, the same guy is in your ear, pumping you up like you're the world champ: "You're a badass." "You're going to dominate out there." "You will win."

What's the story? Is your coach just messing with your head? He's definitely giving you mixed messages, telling you that you're a world-beater *and* that you've got a lot to learn. Well, young grasshopper, that is exactly the message he wants you to hear.

If you want to be a winner, you need to see yourself both ways and learn how to switch from one self-view to the other. As we'll see in this chapter, your ideal training mentality is to see yourself in two ways:

1. Someone who has a lot of work to do
2. Someone who's unstoppable

When you're going into combat, you ought to bring a big ego with you. You're superior to your opponent, and you'll prove it by kicking butt. The more robust your belief in yourself the better (right up to the edge of cockiness). That way you won't get insecure about the gaps in your game or wig out because injuries have left you at less than 100 percent.

If you fall behind in the scorecard, it won't faze you, since you know you'll adjust and come out with the win. And you won't care how tough your opponent is, because you know you're tougher.

But if you carry this arrogance into practice, it works against you. If you think you're already good enough and have nothing more to learn, you won't improve. You'll protest when your coach criticizes you, and you'll both get frustrated. Truly confident people can accept corrective feedback and still maintain a positive view of themselves. In contrast, people who resist constructive criticism are usually hiding a nagging fear that they're not good enough. If you harbor self-doubt, any criticism will bring those doubts to the surface, so you push back.

At the extreme, this takes the form of a narcissist. The narcissist's ego is fragile. All it takes is one example of imperfection to wound them. They therefore push back against the slightest criticism so they can preserve the illusion of perfection and pretend—even to themselves—to be better than they are. Narcissists think their critical coach is trying to break them down. Athletes with a healthy ego think that same coach is trying to make them better.

Gerald Meerschaert, an MMA fighter who holds the record for the most submission wins in the UFC's Middleweight Division, describes himself, especially early in his career, as having "the opposite of an ego problem." He explains that he knew his limitations and tended to worry about an opponent exploiting them.

"I knew what I didn't know," he says. "I was very aware that there were holes in my game and knew that someone might do something that I didn't have an answer for or couldn't accommodate." As he grew more confident, he realized he could succeed despite these gaps, telling himself, "Even with the imperfect skill set I have, I belong here."

Gerald also responded to critical feedback from his coaches differently over time. "When you're constantly being told what you're doing is wrong, you start to think you don't know anything," he says. "Eventually I discovered that I do know what I'm doing, and they're just correcting the small details."

A true champion never stops improving, and this dedication to continuous improvement is one of the keys to greatness. Remember that there's always room for growth because you're never as good as you're capable of being. Even if you're a world champion or a CEO, others will be coming for your title, and you'll have to be better next year than you were this year if you want to stay there.

In the end, we find that most winners are their own harshest critics. Regardless of whether they win or lose, they focus on what they can do better. That's why they're champions.

When we discussed the concept of deliberate practice in Chapter 4, we saw that focusing on your weaknesses is an essential component of proper training. But to turn your weaknesses into strengths, the first step is to recognize your shortcomings. And to do that, you must be honest with yourself.

Growth and Fixed Mindsets

If you favor the "God-given talent" explanation of greatness, you're going to see your slow feet or lack of flexibility as unfortunate restrictions on what you can accomplish. If, however, you believe in your ability to grow and improve, your current limitations are just that: current. They're merely temporary shortcomings that you can overcome with effort.

Psychologist Carol Dweck has labeled these two mindsets as "fixed" and "growth," respectively. In her research, Dweck has found that individuals with a fixed mindset tend to avoid tasks that are difficult for them and give up quickly when they fail. Similarly, they take pride in being able to do something easily—without "trying." People with a fixed mindset are smug about being able to succeed on their first effort and feel superior to those who had to work hard to overcome the same challenge. Having to work hard at something is a source of shame—it means they weren't good enough to do it effortlessly.

In contrast, people with a growth mindset tend to feel proudest when they've had to work their butt off to develop a skill. Let's take the example of a fighter with poor footwork. Their coach correctly suggests they start jumping rope every day. But what if they don't even know how to use the jump rope?

It takes them all morning to make more than one jump in a row, but they persist despite their frustration, and eventually they figure it out. After weeks and then months of jumping rope, they're better at it than most of the team, and their fast feet are now a strong part of their skill set. And each time they jump rope, they feel a sense of pride for having worked hard to get this good. It's also a reminder that, whatever other problems they run into, they can solve them through deliberate practice.

Paul McBeth, the champion disc golfer, describes how some players cease to improve. "There are players that have the raw talent, but they don't put in the time to focus on their weaknesses," he says. "They try to hide their weaknesses with their strengths. They're handicapping themselves, and that's a mental thing."

It can certainly be more fun in the short term to focus on your strengths, but it doesn't help you as much in the long run. Doing the hard work of failing and making adjustments, then failing some more and making more corrections before eventually seeing some improvement—this is how you see long-term success, but it's not always fun. (Remember: One of the defining characteristics of deliberate practice is that it's not inherently fun. It requires us to delay gratification and push through the failures to achieve later and greater success.)

This process is even harder when you have a fixed mindset. If you think that having weaknesses means you've found your ultimate upper limit, you'll play all kinds of tricks on yourself to remain blind to them. By doing so, you'll protect your fragile ego for the moment, but you'll also stay stuck in the mud. If you think your shortcomings aren't fixable, you won't address them, or you'll pretend they don't exist. As a result, your fears become self-fulfilling.

When you lie to yourself in this way, you limit your ability to grow. This is the gist of the insight by famed psychologist Carl Rogers, quoted at the beginning of this chapter. One of the founders of client-centered therapy, Rogers emphasized the concept of congruence, which essentially means being honest with yourself. He believed that your refusal to accept yourself as you are keeps you stuck. When you're in denial, you can't even begin the process of change. But when you're free of fear and shame about yourself, you become congruent and open, and that's when you start to grow.

Implications for Coaches

In the sport context, the concepts covered in this chapter largely determine whether an athlete is "coachable." Coachable athletes are open to feedback because they want to improve, and this desire is stronger than any disappointment they might feel when hearing a coach's criticism. If you're a coach dealing with an athlete who won't listen to you, look into their mindset.

That being said, a coach's approach and demeanor also have a lot to do with the athlete's receptiveness. Especially if you're coaching kids, it's important not to shame them for their lack of skill or ability. If a coach is screaming at a kid or ridiculing them for their mistakes, they'll be motivated to hide their weaknesses. To avoid getting in trouble, they'll rush through their drills to hide their errors or tense up when the coach is watching them. But if the coach promotes a growth mindset and shows patience, the kids will seek out feedback.

The question is not whether you should give corrective feedback as a coach. Of course a good coach is going to be honest with their athletes. The key is to deliver the feedback in a manner that conveys you're trying to help them do better, and you believe they can grow. So don't shame your athletes, but don't coddle them either. Instead, communicate that you approve of them and you want them to improve.

For coaches (and parents), a fundamental way to promote a growth mindset is to praise a child's effort and attitude more than their natural abilities. Attitude and effort are variables they can control, so when you attribute success to these factors, you're conveying that the athlete has agency.

The same goes for criticism. Criticize lack of effort and poor attitudes when you see them, and ideally encourage them to try harder. If you see a kid get taken down for giving up on their shot too quickly, don't scream, "What the heck is wrong with you?" Instead say, "You could have finished that takedown if you stayed with it. Next time I want to see a second, third, and fourth effort."

When a young athlete succeeds early on and is praised for being a "natural," they're likely to believe that their fixed ability is driving their success. This can be a major problem when they inevitably run into a situation or opponent they can't easily overcome. Having come to believe that their natural, fixed talents have gotten them this far, when things get hard, they'll assume they've reached the upper limit of their abilities. They'll think, "I'm not good enough," rather than, "I'm not good enough *yet*."

When you believe the latter, you have the incentive to work toward your goals. Talent can take you part of the way, but you need to work hard as well. As high school basketball coach Tim Notke put it, "Hard work beats talent, until talent decides to work hard."

The Pros and Cons of Perfectionism

Since you'll never be perfect, you'll also never be satisfied. This is the champion's way, but it has risks.

If you're constantly looking at the gap between yourself and perfection, it can demoralize you. No matter how skilled you become, you'll always focus on your flaws. No matter how many wins you rack up, you'll ruminate on your losses. Even when you win, you'll dwell on your mistakes. When you spend every waking moment thinking about the bad stuff, you might start to believe that you're all bad, and this can lead to a dark place. If seeing the gap between where you want to be and where you are now leads to malicious self-criticism, you'll constantly berate yourself, and that's a damaging mindset. In our professional experience, this is one of the most prevalent threats to athletes' mental health.

It's ironic that the best performers are often the most likely to talk about how bad they are, just as the staunchest "clean freak" thinks their spotless home is a mess.

To avoid this trap, you need to consider the nature of your self-talk. In this context, self-talk refers to the messages you give yourself, and it includes both content and tone. One way to think about it is having your own internal coach.

If you constantly tell yourself, "I'm an idiot" when you make a mistake or struggle with a new technique, you can grow to hate yourself. We recommend a more encouraging growth-mindset approach to self-talk. This doesn't require lowering your standards. You can maintain high standards and hold yourself accountable to them without being a jerk to yourself.

Perfectionists are known for having impossibly high standards, and they inevitably disappoint themselves when they fail to meet them. In your case, it's not the high standards that are the problem, but the way you relate to the gap between yourself and perfection.

If you think your imperfections make you a loser, that's a problem. But if your version of perfectionism is striving for perfection while knowing it's an unattainable goal, and you take pleasure in the pursuit, then you'll feel good about yourself throughout the process. You'll never attain perfection, but that's fine—it's the pursuit of perfection that keeps you going. It's the process side of focusing on the process and the outcome.

When Good Enough Is Good Enough

As you enter competitions during your pursuit of perfection, you're aware of your strengths and weaknesses. This is not the time to focus on your weaknesses, but to lean into your strengths and believe in yourself. Like the coach we described at the start of this chapter, who has been on your case all week but then pumps you up going into a fight, you should now see yourself as good enough to dominate your opponent.

The paradox here is that you've gone through your training with the mindset that you're not good enough and need to get better. But it's precisely this "never good enough" training mentality that makes you good enough to dominate in competition. Because you've gotten better every day during training, you're good enough to win.

In the midst of combat, focusing on your shortcomings can be fatal to your self-confidence. You've already got an opponent trying to beat you, so you don't need to beat yourself through self-doubt. It's a good idea to forget your faults. That doesn't mean you should take foolish risks in situations where your opponent has an edge—just have confidence in yourself where you fully expect to win. You've trained like crazy, so you've earned this right.

Solid evidence shows that your belief in your ability to succeed, or lack thereof, becomes self-fulfilling. We've all heard the adage "If you think you can or think you can't—you're right." Many experiments have shown that if you manipulate a person's belief that they will succeed at a task, you can affect the outcome, even though their innate ability hasn't changed.

In 1954, English athlete Roger Bannister became the first person to run a mile in less than 4 minutes. That limit had been considered insurmountable for many years, but once Bannister showed it was possible, several other runners soon duplicated the feat, including Australian runner John Landy just 46 days later. Since then, more than 1,400 runners have run a 4-minute mile. The barrier was more a mental than a physical one, and once Bannister proved it could be done, the barrier was broken. If you believe in your ability to win, regardless of your physical limitations, you increase your chances of victory.

How far should you go with this self-belief and forgetting your faults? If you're a great wrestler in an MMA fight with a superior striker, standing and trading with them could be foolish. The wiser and safer option would be to get the fight to the ground, where you have the clear advantage. Yet we can argue that showing confidence in your own striking, even if it's a bit inflated, can become a self-fulfilling prophecy. You know your opponent's skills, but if you believe your striking prowess is good enough, that helps you fight with the sense of purpose and confidence you need. You shouldn't be timid just because your opponent has the advantage "on paper." And remember that your adversary is dealing with their own mental battles. If you show them you're afraid, it will boost their confidence, but if you take the fight to them on your feet, you can sow the seeds of doubt in their mind.

There is no clearer example of this mentality than Chris Weidman's knockout victory over Anderson Silva to claim the middleweight title at UFC 162 in 2013. Going into the fight, Silva was by all accounts deemed the superior striker—indeed, he was considered by many experts the best MMA striker of all time. Yet Weidman would not be intimidated. "I refused to feel that I had no ability to be there with him on my feet," he says. Recalling his mindset going in, Weidman says, "I know he's really good, but I'm sparring with all these top boxers. I believe in my standup, too."

Clearly, Weidman leveraged his training to bolster his confidence, regardless of where the fight went. "The main thing for me in that fight was to not hold back anything—to let my instincts go," he says. "I wanted to get the fight to the ground, but I didn't want to be insecure on my feet." He knew his own strengths and weaknesses relative to his opponent, but he also knew he was good enough to win. "My plan was to be constantly in his face, and I knew eventually he'll break somehow," he says. "That mindset is what got me the finish."

Weidman's iconic victory is just one case of the underdog beating an opponent who is supposedly the better fighter; there are many others. When you believe in yourself, you can do incredible things. It doesn't matter what the public thinks or what's "supposed" to happen. If you believe you're good enough, you're bound to be right.

And this belief in yourself extends to all kinds of setbacks and obstacles that come your way. Perhaps you have an injury and can't grip with your right hand. Or you couldn't spar as much as you wanted to and don't feel as sharp as you should. Or you're feeling a bit sick going into a match and might get fatigued.

If your confidence is fragile, any of these things can become excuses, but with a deep belief in yourself, nothing will derail you. When asked about dealing with injuries or taking a short-notice fight, Weidman says, "When you're in those moments, a part of you wants to give yourself an excuse to lose. It's a self-talk battle inside of me, but I tell myself 'No, no. I have to win. There's no excuses.'"

With a winner's mindset, you can be imperfect in all sorts of ways and still be good enough to get the job done. As legendary basketball coach John Wooden said, "Do not let what you cannot do interfere with what you can do."

So believe in yourself. Be proud of who you are. You are good enough to be out there doing what you're doing. And, lest we forget, you need to keep getting better. Immediately after capturing the UFC belt, Weidman was asked at the post-fight press conference what happens next for him. He said, "It's crazy. I would think I'd sit back and relax, but instantly, I'm hungry. I need to get better. I feel like I still didn't look my best." Even when you're the champion of the world, you need to keep improving.

CHAPTER 8

Respecting Your Opponent AND Crushing Your Opponent

Respecting Your Opponent

Pros

- Promotes sportsmanship and goodwill
- Prevents "letting your guard down"
- Provides a strong source of motivation

Cons

- Can inhibit your killer instinct
- At extremes, leads to hesitation and fear
- Takes the focus off your own goals

When to Use This Attitude

- Before and after competition
- To counter your complacency
- When you're taking someone lightly

Crushing Your Opponent

Pros

- Enhances motivation
- Promotes an extra level of intensity
- Increases your intimidation factor

Cons

- Can lead to poor sportsmanship
- May isolate you from others
- Can lead to underestimating opponents

When to Use This Attitude

- At competition time
- When you need a motivation boost
- To intimidate your opponents

Respecting Your Opponent AND Crushing Your Opponent: Pros, Cons, and When to Use

"If you even dream of beating me, you'd better wake up and apologize."

—Muhammad Ali

"We do not train to be merciful here. Mercy is for the weak.
Here, on the streets, in competition, a man confronts you,
he is the enemy. An enemy deserves no mercy."

—John Kreese (played by actor Martin Kove), *The Karate Kid*

Steve Mocco, a two-time NCAA wrestling champion, Olympian, professional MMA fighter, and coach, had an experience at a youth tournament that proved to be a formative one for him. He had become friends with an opponent before a match, and he lost.

"In my head, I lost because I befriended him, because I wasn't going into combat with him," says Steve, whose story is detailed in the FloWrestling series *Mocco*.

As he grew into a more seasoned competitor, Steve adopted a more combative attitude: "Anybody I competed against I took as a threat."

While the previous chapter focused on your relationship with yourself, this one centers on your relationship with your opponents—seeing them as both your worst enemies and your greatest allies.

At times you should treat your opponents with the utmost respect, and at other times it's best to treat them with disdain. Especially in an individual sport or during a one-on-one matchup in a team sport, they are directly trying to prevent you from achieving your goals. If they win, they will take something from you—your advancement to the next round, your prize money, or your belt.

They don't care about you, and you shouldn't care about them. When the whistle blows, it's about you and what you want. To heck with the other guy.

But what if you flipped that way of thinking a bit?

If not for your opponent, you wouldn't even have the opportunity to compete, and in that sense, he's your partner.

Sport psychologist Michael Johnson points out that the word "compete" comes from the original Latin word *competere*, formed from the prefix *com*, meaning "together," and *petere*, meaning "to seek or strive for." "Even as you compete against an opponent, you are both, quite literally, striving together," Johnson says. Champions love to push themselves to become greater than they are, and there is no better way to do that than to face off against a challenging rival. "Iron sharpens iron," as the proverb says. Your fiercest competitors are also your greatest motivators. Respect them for it.

If you've ever been in a hard-fought battle, you know the feeling of both loving and hating your opponent. One moment you're trying to knock each other's head off, and the next you're hugging it out and thanking each other for making the contest possible. (Think about the iconic handshake lines at the end of playoff hockey games.)

This phenomenon of tough competitors making each other better is leveraged every day in gyms and dojos and wrestling rooms. Coaches and trainers work hard to recruit great training partners for their best athletes, and those athletes choose to train where they will be pushed by in-house competition. It's no coincidence that the two best combatants on a team are often at adjacent weight classes. They're going to war with each other every day.

Or look at the champions found among brothers and sisters, especially twins. The wrestling world is chock full of them, such as the fraternal pairs of Banach, Peterson, Schultz, Beloglazov, Brands, and Ben's own brother Max Askren. In tennis, it's Venus and Serena Williams, Jamie and Andy Murray, and siblings Marat Safin and Dinara Safina. If you want to maximize your training, you may not be able to create a sibling, but you can seek out the toughest competition every day.

The concept of striving together through competition is, in fact, the reason we have sport in the first place. The ancients created sporting events to prepare soldiers for war because they knew the best way to improve their skills was by competing among themselves. That's why ancient sporting events reflected the skills required of soldiers at the time. The ancient pentathlon, for example, called for running, jumping, discus and javelin throwing, and wrestling. The best athlete was nearly synonymous with the best warrior. And certain events, such as the *hoplitodromos*, even required the competitors to run a race with their helmets, armor, and shields. Although most athletes today are not explicitly competing as a way to prepare for war, the harder two training partners compete against each other, the better prepared they will be for the actual competition.

Respect Inside and Outside Competition

In competition, you and your foe are partners in opposition, and the best way to show mutual respect is to devote yourselves fully to crushing each other. You need to bring all your resources to bear to accomplish this goal. Use your strength, your cunning, and your gamesmanship to defeat them.

Do everything you can within the confines of the rules, and perhaps even bending the rules, to make them pay for trying to beat you. Don't just settle for the win, either. Whomever you're fighting, you might see them again, so beat them so badly that the thought of facing you once more mentally defeats them before the next fight even starts.

There is debate in some circles about how far to take this mindset of crushing your opponent. Especially in team sports, coaches are often criticized for running up the score. Governing bodies create "mercy rules" that lead to a running clock when a lead becomes too great or ending a match when "technical superiority" is achieved. But what if there is no escape, and your opponent is being humiliated by your success?

With the exception of youth sports, where athletes' social and emotional development can be a higher priority than the competition, we strongly favor continuing to crush them until the final horn. During the battle, it's not your job to care for your opponent's emotional needs. The two of you entered into competition with an understanding that you would compete to the best of your ability, and that should be your singular focus. Taking it easy on them out of pity could be seen as a sign of disrespect.

This changes, however, when the fight is over. That is the time to empathize, to see in your adversary a reflection of yourself—

someone who works hard in pursuit of their own goals and who, just like you, rides the emotional highs and lows of success and failure.

If you've won, be humble in victory.

If you've lost, be gracious in defeat.

During competition, your opponent is your adversary. But before and after, your relationship need not be adversarial. You should also remember that sometimes the person who is your opponent today becomes your teammate tomorrow. If you carry around your disdain for your opponents outside the competition, you'll create obstacles to learning from them and helping each other improve.

How Much Respect Is Enough?

Looking at the original meaning of *respect* (as we did with *competition*) can be revealing. It comes from the Latin *respicere*, which is composed of the prefix *re*, meaning "back," and the root word *specere*, meaning "to look." So *respect* literally means "to look back." When you show someone respect, you are looking back at them or seeing them.

To decide whether to respect an opponent or crush them, we've focused on seeing them as a person with thoughts and feelings before and after competition vs. not seeing this at all during competition. It's a matter of switching from seeing to not seeing. But there's another way to think about respect within the competitive arena, where our challenge is not so much deciding whether to see our opponent, but rather to see them (i.e., respect them) the *right amount*.

Here we're referring to another connotation of the word *respect*, such as, "You need to respect the power in his right hand," or "You're showing him too much respect." We're still talking about seeing or paying attention to your opponent, but now by focusing on them as a threat. If you see them as too much of a threat, you'll be hesitant and fight scared. If you see them as too little of a threat, you'll take foolish risks and get caught with your hands down. We're aiming for a balance of respecting your opponent—but not too much.

Some athletes learn their opponent's reputation and concede defeat before the contest begins. That's too much respect. If you have this problem, you're better off not paying any attention to your opponents' records or accolades. We've seen novice athletes go out and take a lead on a supposedly superior opponent while they have no idea who they're up against. Then, during a break in the action, someone screws it up by saying, "Wow, I can't believe you're beating this guy. He's a state champion." Having learned they're not "supposed to be" winning, they promptly blow their lead.

One of Ben's wrestling protégés, Keegan O'Toole, fell victim to this trap while facing Beau Bartlett in the 2018 U17 World Team Trials. Bartlett was widely considered the favorite in the weight class and the top prospect in the country, but midway through the match Keegan was ahead 5-1. During the break, doubt crept in, and when the action resumed, instead of reengaging with a wrestler he was clearly beating, Keegan was mentally battling his opponent's reputation. Keegan began wrestling defensively, as if he was lucky to be ahead, and Beau took advantage of that to secure a 7-5 comeback win.

It was a tough loss to swallow—he was beaten because he gave his opponent too much respect. Fortunately, Keegan, with his coach's help, took his medicine and learned from the experience. As of this writing, he has won a junior world championship and two NCAA titles.

Other athletes have too little respect for their opponents' skills. Believing too much in their own superiority, they fail to see their opponents as any threat at all, clown around, and end up getting caught. Never expect someone to roll over for you. Take every opponent seriously.

Finding the proper amount of respect for your opponent is very much a corollary to achieving the ideal amount of confidence in yourself—you should firmly believe you can win, but only if you try hard. Similarly, showing adequate (but not too much) respect for your opponent means knowing they can beat you if you slack off, but they can't defeat you at your best.

Respecting your opponents in this way also helps you make real-time adjustments to your game plan. If your approach isn't working, it could be due to your poor execution, but it also might be because your opponent is doing a great job. When two competitors are evenly matched, the victory goes to the one who adjusts to the situation better. And to adapt and overcome, you must respect your opponent.

CHAPTER 9

Preparing for Everything AND Expecting the Unexpected

Preparing for Everything

Pros
- Minimizes situations that will rattle you
- Encourages thorough training
- Promotes confidence and game-planning

Cons
- Confusion when the unexpected occurs
- Can lead to obsessive-compulsiveness
- Makes it hard to be spontaneous

When to Use This Attitude
- During training and preparation
- When game-planning
- When learning and drilling technique

Expecting the Unexpected

Pros
- Promotes spontaneity
- Reduces anxiety
- Fosters an "adapt and overcome" attitude

Cons
- Can lead to complacency in preparation
- May limit an "impose your will" mentality
- Can lead to a reactive approach

When to Use This Attitude
- As unforeseen obstacles arise
- When sparring and "play-fighting"
- Always, in the back of your mind

Preparing for Everything AND Expecting the Unexpected: Pros, Cons, and When to Use

"If you fail to prepare, you are preparing to fail."

—Author unknown

"The essence of neurosis is the inability to tolerate ambiguity."

—Sigmund Freud, psychoanalyst

As we all know, there's no substitute for preparation. The best athletes come ready when it's time to perform.

They obsess about training and details. They learn and refine their technical skills, and they work on their strength, endurance, and flexibility. They eat right, sleep well, and study their opponents (even finding opponents whose style mimics them). They do it all.

Yet no amount of planning or visualization will allow you to control everything. As University of Pittsburgh wrestling coach Keith Gavin puts it, "You can't control the outcome; you can only have influence over it."

That's because real life—and opponents' actions—requires you to adapt to different situations, using more than one approach to accomplish a goal.

Well-prepared competitors need to consider all the different ways a contest can go and plan for every contingency. Otherwise, they risk being one-dimensional (a disadvantage in unpredictable battles).

But here's the rub (there's always a rub): In sport and combat, it's impossible to predict and prepare for everything, so you also need to get comfortable with the unknown and learn to expect the unexpected.

Dominique Moceanu, the champion gymnast and coach, says, "You train as hard as you can to stack the deck in your favor, and that will give you confidence as well, but you never know what's going to happen. You have to prepare for everything, as much as possible, that's in your control, and then you have to give up control once you get there and let the chips fall where they may."

Without this ability to adapt, an injury that interrupts your training plan can be devastating. If you're a serious athlete gearing up for an important competition, you've likely mapped out your workouts in detail. The last thing you want to do is take any time off, for any reason. But stuff happens.

Ben faced this exact dilemma in 2007. In the course of winning the Big 12 Conference wrestling title, he injured his ribs. With about three weeks to go until the NCAA championships, his choices were either to keep training as planned and risk making the injury worse or to avoid heavy drilling and sparring, thus entering the national tournament in less-than-ideal shape and form.

He ultimately decided he'd have a better chance of winning the title out of shape than injured, so he opted to rest his ribs. We'll explore the nuts and bolts of handling injuries in Chapter 11, but our focus here is how Ben handled the situation emotionally. Rather than pouting about his misfortune or ruminating on how it was throwing off his training regimen, he accepted the reality that he was hurt, adapted to this unexpected event, and made the best of the situation. He eventually won the NCAA title despite his training setback, as well as the Dan Hodge trophy for the most outstanding college wrestler in any weight class.

An injury that occurs prior to a competition allows the athlete extra time and consultation with others to decide how to respond. But when the unexpected occurs during competition, you must adapt immediately.

Ben has faced these situations as well. (When you compete long enough, you accrue an extended list of bizarre and unforeseen obstacles.) In the semifinals of a tournament in Ukraine in 2008, Ben was leading with six seconds left in the final period when wrestling resumed. As the seconds ticked off—or so he thought—Ben was sure the match should be over. He glanced over at the clock and saw that it hadn't started. In that brief moment of distraction, his opponent scored and won the match. There was clearly a technical error, but the officials refused to review it. It was a lesson learned: Never look away under any circumstances and wrestle until you hear the whistle. Anything can happen, and the one who adapts most quickly and effectively is the one who comes out on top.

MMA fighter Gerald Meerschaert began competing in 2007, when events weren't always run in the most organized fashion. "I've probably warmed up in the utensils closet of a bar kitchen at least 10 times to get ready for a cage fight," he says. "The thing was, it forced me to learn to compete in subpar conditions."

That adaptability paid dividends during Gerald's first UFC fight in 2016, when the fight card was running behind schedule. The organizers tried to speed things along by walking the on-deck fighters out to the Octagon while the prior fight was still in progress. Of course, this interrupted everyone's warm-up routine, which played to Gerald's advantage. "We had to stand there next to the crowd in front of the cage, but I was so used to warming up in weird situations that it didn't really faze me at all," he says. "It helped a lot, and I ended up finishing that fight and getting a bonus."

Gerald notes that as a coach and cornerman, he often sees other fighters struggle when something small goes wrong, such as a shortage of gauze or tape in the training room. His experience tells him to expect these problems, and during his fighting career he came prepared, even when he was not scheduled to fight. "Back in the day, you never knew when someone might drop out and you'd have to hop in there and fight someone," he says.

Gerald's composure translates into his fighting style, and he is known as someone who thrives in unpredictability. "I want to force you into these chaotic scrambles, where I've been there so often and am so comfortable that even though it looks nuts, I'm still flowing and knowing what I'm supposed to be doing," he says.

When Chris Weidman received his first opportunity to fight in the UFC in 2011, against Alessio Sakara, he had just over two weeks to prepare. He was also dealing with broken ribs at the time, so he was unable to spar leading up to the fight. Chris explains, "It was risky, but this was my opportunity," and he made the most of it by securing the unanimous decision win.

Chris faced a similar situation the following year when he received an offer to fight Demian Maia on just 10 days' notice. This time he wasn't injured—but he was 32 pounds overweight. Not ideal, but he again jumped at the unexpected chance to face off against a world-class fighter. "He was ranked fifth in the world, and this was my opportunity to get into the top echelon of the division, so I decided I'm doing this," Chris says. Once again, his decision to fight paid off with a unanimous decision victory.

Chris acknowledges that these choices don't always work out. In a 2016 fight against Yoel Romero, he competed after injuring his knee (and undergoing surgery) less than a month before the fight. Weidman lost that contest, yet his commitment to competing in his home state of New York, where he had actively lobbied to gain sanctioning for MMA, meant that no unexpected hiccup would dissuade him. "I couldn't shadowbox or move around, because the knee was swollen," he recalls. "But there was no way I was backing out."

For those athletes who want to prepare for everything and tightly control their training regimen, competing while injured or without adequate time to prepare seems foolish. Under ideal circumstances, you certainly should do everything right and exhibit an unwavering commitment to your daily grind and habits.

Yet taken to the extreme, this approach can become obsessive-compulsive disorder (OCD). For those suffering with OCD, living in an uncertain world is scary, and the way to make it tolerable is to control everything you can.

In the context of a sport, this means counting calories, monitoring fluid intake, getting the requisite number of reps in, and excluding anything that will distract you from your routine. All it takes is one unexpected hiccup to throw you off: a sore shoulder, a slight cold, a traffic jam that cuts 5 minutes off your gym time. At nondisordered levels, all this looks like solid self-discipline. But if you don't manage these tendencies, your mental attitude becomes fragile, and your careful planning becomes a crutch. You'll feel good about your chances only as long as you can control everything, turn down a last-minute fight because you couldn't complete a proper training camp, and pull out of a fight due to a nagging injury. When something goes awry, you'll see it as a crisis, and anxiety, trouble sleeping, and neuroses can follow. As Sigmund Freud said in one of this chapter's opening quotes, being unable to tolerate an ambiguous world is the definition of neurosis.

There's a fine line between caring deeply about your sport and being pathological about it. Georges St-Pierre, one of the greatest mixed martial artists of all time, is known for his incredible work ethic and disciplined approach to every aspect of his craft. He has also divulged that he's struggled with OCD. Speaking with the CBC's Wendy Mesley in 2014, he explained the benefits and drawbacks of an obsessive-compulsive mindset. "As a fighter it's a good thing to have it, because it makes you better because you completely obsess about being a better martial artist. But the same obsession I have about my job was going to make me crazy."

We recommend being extremely disciplined, even borderline obsessive, under most circumstances, but shifting to a c'est la vie mindset when the unexpected occurs. This is not, of course, advocating for switching to a completely carefree attitude or abandoning your plans at the first sign of adversity.

For example, if your ride to practice falls through, the solution is not just to skip practice that day. First, consider other ways to get there. If that fails, you can figure out an alternative workout. Likewise, if you plan to get a full 8 hours of sleep so you can train hard in the morning, getting invited to a cool party isn't a good reason to stay up. Sleep is important, so go to bed. But if you can't sleep because the fire alarm keeps going off, that doesn't mean your training session is ruined. You can still get there and be ready to go, notwithstanding your sleep debt. Even if you do slip and end up partying instead of resting, don't waste time kicking yourself over your poor choice. What's done is done, and you can adapt by pushing through and doing better the next day—or the next night, as the case may be.

For those with a high level of anxiety or a strong ego orientation, something going unexpectedly wrong can actually lower their burden and lead to better performance. Rather than viewing an injury as a threat to their success, for example, they may experience it as ironically calming. In this case an injury can pull the anxious competitor out of their ego orientation and into a task-oriented mindset (see Chapter 6), which lowers their anxiety and helps them focus on the task at hand.

Many of the less disciplined athletes who both work hard and play hard have one advantage over their more anxious, more disciplined peers: a robust confidence that's not shaken by a misstep or change in plans. They don't see one late night or one slice of pizza as a threat to their success, and they won't have a meltdown over a minor injury or schedule change. They know "stuff happens," and they don't let the details bog them down.

Sometimes these two extreme personality types end up on the same team. That's when their coaches wish they could combine the two, so that a bit of the disciplined workhorse would rub off on the happy-go-lucky athlete, and a bit of the free spirit would help the serious-minded one mellow out. That way, both of them would make thoughtful, goal-oriented choices while rolling with the punches.

Speaking of coaches, they, too, must find a balance between preparing for everything and expecting the unexpected. Dan Gable says he both planned and adapted throughout his coaching career. "I would go to practice every day, and I spent a good 30 minutes with a practice plan every day," he says. "I never once finished that practice plan in 25 years. I didn't start and finish like I wrote it out because things happen, and you have to adjust to get the most out of the athletes." In addition to spurring his wrestlers to get the most out of practice each day, Dan was modeling both sides of the dichotomy for them: establishing the importance of being prepared with a deliberate plan every day as well as the value of adapting to the unexpected.

Adaptability is, in itself, a skill—one that is every bit as valuable as your technical skills and your fitness, although it's more of a mental or attitudinal skill than a physical one. Just as you can train for strength, speed, and endurance, you can train to develop your adaptability.

You can learn it through observing others or by having a coach or trainer who throws curveballs at you at unpredictable times, such as switching practice partners on you, making you spar with one eye covered, or unfairly withholding points in a practice match, thus forcing you into simulated overtime. After all, you never know when your eye might swell shut in a fight or a referee might make a bad call in your opponent's favor. Simulating such events in practice can help you adapt quickly when they occur during competition.

Be an Artist and a Scientist

While "preparing for everything" requires a scientific approach, "expecting the unexpected" calls for a more artistic mindset.

In training and competition, the ideal athlete employs both artistic and scientific principles. In a practice session, instruction and drilling are the science: There are right and wrong ways to do things, and the main focus when learning a skill is to get it right. The process typically involves an expert demonstrating the proper technique and then having the learner drill that technique with perfect form repeatedly, correcting any mistakes or imperfections along the way. This process is essential for developing expertise, but it's not sufficient.

To become an expert in a dynamic sport, which requires you to adapt as you go, you need to train as an artist as well. Sparring, for example, calls for a more artistic approach. In sparring, two partners engage in a partly competitive, somewhat playful interaction to help each other develop their skills. The proportion of competitive vs. cooperative efforts they make is, in itself, rather artfully determined. When good training partners spar, it's as much a dance as a competition. Typically, one assumes the role of learner while the other takes the role of opponent-teacher. The latter is not trying to win, but to provide the learner with a realistic competition, so they can add an artistic expertise to their scientifically learned techniques.

We're using the term "sparring" here to refer to any situation in which the partner is offering resistance, as opposed to drilling, in which the partner is more of a passive "dummy" on whom the learner practices. It can range from light sparring (which some casually call drilling as well), in which the partner offers very minimal resistance, perhaps no more than positional reactions, to heavy sparring, in which both athletes are exerting close to maximal effort. We could say that sparring is akin to "play fighting," and lots of creative solutions emerge out of play.

When teammates have reached a dance-partner level of understanding, they intuitively know how much resistance to offer. They often talk to each other (e.g., "Make me work a bit to get to the inside" or "Don't let me control your wrist"), but often their communication is unspoken. This process helps athletes develop their artistic feel and learn how to execute their "book knowledge," if you will, in competition. The more athletes experience different reactions through sparring, the more they develop the ability to adjust on the fly and improvise in competition. While drilling is largely a conscious process, sparring allows you to hone an athlete's many unconscious decisions and movements.

A scientist uses established knowledge and proven techniques when conducting a planned experiment or study. Many athletes, along with their coaches, correctly use a scientific approach when game-planning for a specific opponent. They study their opponent's habits and tendencies and devise a strategy to overcome them, using established techniques that have been shown to work in a particular scenario. This is wise. But when they encounter unanticipated situations—that's when they must be an artist. At those moments, they go with what "feels right," rely on their instincts, and derive a solution on the spot. They improvise.

This is not to say that one approach is superior to the other—both approaches are essential. When someone invents a move out of necessity during competition, they will review and analyze what happened to figure out why it worked before incorporating it into the ever-evolving science of the sport. Today's creative technique becomes tomorrow's daily drill.

There is a reason we call them the martial *arts*. The arts and sciences may seem distinct, but the champion is both an artist and a scientist. The two are separate, but complementary.

Impose Your Will and Adapt to Your Opponent

You can benefit enormously from going into a competition with a game plan in mind, but you also need the confidence and tenacity to stick to that plan when your opponent puts up a fight. If you abandon it at the first sign of resistance, you'll never defeat a worthy adversary. You need to impose your will.

Take this principle to the extreme, however, and tenacity becomes stubbornness. That's when you might end up focusing more on executing your game plan than on the game itself. If your opponent has an answer for you, the wise choice is to adapt so you can overcome and adjust your strategy as you go. Knowing when to persevere and when to adjust is a major key to success.

The concept of being tough-smart rather than tough-stupid (see Figure 2.3 on page 31) applies here. A tough-stupid competitor will stick to their plan even if it's not working. Imposing their will at all costs is more important than getting the win. We see this often in MMA when, for example, a fighter attempts a takedown and the opponent defends it. Instead of transitioning to another finishing technique or returning to a neutral, standing position, the aggressor hangs on to the opponent's leg and gets repeatedly punched as a consequence for his stubbornness. The tough-smart person keeps their eye on the goal and adapts when their initial plan fails. If a takedown attempt is defended, they adjust and try again with a different setup or from a different angle. You can find a balance between giving up on a position too early (which would be wimpy) vs. hanging on too long, which is true for any strategy.

If your plan isn't working, you don't want to abandon it immediately, but you also want to be flexible and respond to what your opponent is giving you. A big part of the "art" in martial arts is managing the give-and-take between offensively imposing your will and defensively adapting to your opponent.

Different martial arts emphasize different parts of this dichotomy. Wrestlers are typically trained to favor offense and impose their will tenaciously. They do well when the contest comes down to a battle of wills. At the other extreme, aikido practitioners emphasize harmony and unity. They are skilled at quickly ascertaining their adversary's intent and adapting to it. People frequently argue about which approach is the best base for a mixed martial artist, but champions recognize that every tradition has value. By studying multiple arts, they have a diverse toolkit from which to draw, and much of their skill lies in choosing the best approach for the situation at hand.

In any form of combat, there's a constant back-and-forth between the opponents, with tiny adjustments in force, angles, and pressure. To the untrained eye, it might look like they are simply pushing on each other or just staring each other down, but they are actually engaged in a dance of countless nuanced adaptations that occur in a matter of milliseconds, largely on an unconscious level. When you're well-trained, you can do so expertly.

CHAPTER 10

Using Your Head AND Using Your Instinct

Using Your Head

Pros
- Allows for intelligent decision making
- Promotes skill development
- Leads to effective strategizing

Cons
- Is a relatively slow process
- Can lead to "analysis paralysis"
- Requires much cognitive effort

When to Use This Attitude
- When learning a new skill
- When strategic adjustments are needed
- In pre- and post-competition analysis

Using Your Instinct

Pros
- Is a fast and efficient process
- Keeps you "out of your own head"
- Allows for creative, improvised solutions

Cons
- Can keep you blind to relevant information
- Limits smart decision making
- Prevents effective learning

When to Use This Attitude
- When performing well-known skills
- In sparring and competition
- When under time pressure

Using Your Head AND Using Your Instinct: Pros, Cons, and When to Use

"You don't have time to think up there. If you think, you're dead."

—Maverick (played by actor Tom Cruise), *Top Gun*

Expert performance requires a combination of conscious, deliberate thought and the ability to perform automatically, without thinking. You need both conscious and unconscious control. When we introduced the premise about using both mindsets in Chapter 1, we briefly described the autonomic and somatic nervous systems. In this chapter, we will be delving into them more deeply, as they factor heavily in the process of thinking and not thinking, depending on the task.

As a general guide, when you're learning a new skill or correcting imperfections in your technique (i.e., when you're in learning mode and using the "beginner's mind" mentality), you should use your head. This puts your somatic nervous system in the driver's seat, so you can think carefully about how the technique works, focus on the details, ask questions, and even take notes. The learning phase requires a great deal of attention and cognitive effort, so it's helpful to take things slow and make sure you get it right.

Once you've mastered a technique and can execute it correctly and consistently, it's best not to think about it and just let your autonomic nervous system do its thing. With much deliberate practice, complex skills that initially required a lot of attention and mental energy become automated. Thinking too much at this stage slows you down and decreases your efficiency. In competition, you should trust your training and let your body do what it "knows" how to do unconsciously.

"You've got to learn enough to know enough, but then shut it off and get to that flow state," says MMA champion Gerald Meerschaert. "All the thinking should have been done in training. In a fight, I don't want to be thinking. I want to be reacting."

Many athletes, for various reasons, are impatient in the learning process. They try a technique once or twice and then try to execute it quickly, as if they've nailed it down. But rushing through a new technique only lets you hide your mistakes. You're likely doing it imperfectly, and by not slowing down enough to give deliberate thought and attention to the details, you're incorporating incorrect technique into your repertoire.

This habit is the bane of coaches' existence, who often complain about having to "unteach" kids the wrong way to do things so they can teach them the correct way instead. The early learning phase is the time to pause, adjust, and ask a coach for feedback when you're having trouble getting it.

Then, once you've learned how to do it perfectly, you repeat the skill, drilling it correctly many times. As you start getting the right "feel" of the technique, you can add speed to your drills. With enough repetitions—and we're talking hundreds or thousands here—you develop a "muscle memory" for it and can execute it without much conscious thought. Only then is it preferable not to think, but just act. It's similar to the transition from drilling (more scientific) to sparring (more artistic), which we covered in the previous chapter. .

In reality, you are using your autonomic and somatic nervous systems simultaneously, at least when you're awake. You are conscious of some things—that is, you are deliberately paying attention to them—while doing many other things at an unconscious level. One important aspect of expertise is directing your conscious thoughts to the tasks and decisions that require your attention, while letting your unconscious handle the things that are best done by instinct.

Conscious and Unconscious Control

The autonomic system, which operates outside your conscious control, responds without having to exert any real willpower or intention. It keeps your heart beating, your pupils contracting and dilating, and guides your instinctive reactions. The somatic system, by comparison, operates whenever you consciously decide to move or speak. When you get dressed, lift weights, stretch out, or do anything at all with deliberate intent, you're using your somatic nervous system. It operates far more slowly than the autonomic system. Although you can train yourself to move faster and increase your reaction speed, your instinctive or autonomic reactions are exponentially faster.

If you're in a fight and your opponent's fist is flying toward your head, you don't have time to analyze your options for evading or blocking the blow. If you take even a split second to think about it, you're likely to get knocked out. You'd be using your somatic/voluntary nervous system when your autonomic system should be in charge—or in other words, you'd be thinking instead of doing, a phenomenon often called "analysis paralysis."

If the story ended there, we could simply tell you not to think during combat; just act. Of course, it's not so simple, since there are also times when acting without thinking can be a problem. Picture an MMA fighter who's knocked his opponent down and has a perfect opening to deliver a knee to the head. His instinct is to fire it off and end the fight right there. But there's a rule against kicking or kneeing a downed opponent in the head, so our fighter needs to use his voluntary nervous system to stop his autonomic response and pick another option: maybe an elbow to the head or a knee to the ribcage. If he doesn't pause to think, he could lose the fight due to disqualification.

Other situations require unconscious control, as we've seen, and many situations require a combination of both. Let's look at our MMA fighter again. This time he's trying to land a multiple-punch combination. He's not consciously telling himself how to turn his wrist, or where his feet should be when he throws, or which muscles to flex. He doesn't need to remind himself of all the steps involved. When it's time, he just needs to act.

That being said, he does need to engage his conscious mind to decide *when* to execute. His coaches told him between rounds that his opponent has been dropping his hands after throwing a low kick, and our fighter is now consciously watching for that tendency and making decisions accordingly. But as he is analyzing and thinking about when to respond to an opening, his unconscious or autonomic system is keeping his other actions going on autopilot.

Speaking of getting advice during a fight, a word or two is in order regarding a coach's role as it pertains to an athlete's conscious and unconscious control. Since conscious control requires time and mental energy, and both are limited resources for a combatant, coaches should be careful to limit the technical advice they give their athletes immediately before and during competition. Most highly experienced coaches will tell you to offer no more than two or three instructions; more, and the athlete could get overwhelmed and run into analysis paralysis.

These concepts serve as the guiding themes of one of the most influential and widely read books on the mental aspects of performance, *The Inner Game of Tennis* by W. Timothy Gallwey. That book, as well as other books in the author's *Inner Game* series, describes two selves that are constantly interacting with each other. Gallwey noticed that players continuously talk to themselves, which necessarily implies that there are two parts operating simultaneously: the one doing the talking and the other doing the listening. He labels the part that does the telling "Self 1" and calls the part that performs the action "Self 2." Galway states, "The key to better tennis—or better anything—lies in improving the relationship between the conscious teller, Self 1, and the natural capabilities of Self 2."

Gallwey derived his approach largely from his work as a professional tennis coach, where he found that the solution to players' technical problems often came through nontechnical suggestions. When someone needed help with a bad swing, rather than focusing on the specific mechanics of the player's execution, which would promote conscious attention on the many skills involved (e.g., where to place your thumb, when to bend your elbow rather than your wrist), he would offer more general advice.

For example, he might tell a player to aim farther back on the court. This occupied their conscious system with thoughts of ball placement and created space for the unconscious system of "Self 2" to handle the nuances of hitting a moving target by swinging a racket. In what often seems like magic, your body figures out on its own what it needs to do.

When you look more closely at all the processes involved in a complex skill such as hitting a ball with a racket, throwing a combination of strikes, or even getting up out of a chair, you find that an inordinate number of separate physical actions have to be coordinated. If you had to consciously think about all of them, it would be cognitively exhausting. Fortunately, you don't have to. For the vast majority of your movements, there is an unconscious, fast-thinking system coordinating things behind the scenes, allowing your slower-thinking conscious system to focus on other matters.

The concept of separate fast- and slow-thinking systems has been illuminated by psychologists Daniel Kahneman and Amos Tversky. Kahneman was awarded the Nobel Prize in Economic Sciences for their work in 2002. (Tversky had died in 1996, and the Nobel is not awarded posthumously.) In his 2011 book *Thinking, Fast and Slow*, Kahneman provides detailed explanations of these two systems and of the various ways they operate and affect our actions and choices. One major and well-established finding is that your fast-thinking, largely unconscious system, which he calls "System 1," handles the vast majority of the decisions you make throughout the day, which number in the tens of thousands. This allows your slow-thinking "System 2" to focus on tasks that require cognitive effort, such as solving a math problem or writing a sentence. Although we commonly refer to System 2's functions as "thinking" and System 1's efforts as "actions," Kahneman explains that it's all thinking, just in different ways. So when a coach tells you, "Don't think, just act," they're really telling you to stay with the fast-thinking approach of System 1.

Especially in fast-paced, demanding settings like sport, staying in System 1 provides a solid advantage. Elite performers can act and react ostensibly without effort, even in the most complex situations, in a way that seems unfathomable to a novice. How is this possible? Do they simply have some "God-given talent" that the rest of us lack?

Although many spectators assume so and comfort themselves by declaring, "I could never do that," the evidence shows that, with enough deliberate practice, complex tasks that initially require us to use our conscious, slow-thinking System 2 can become fast-thinking System 1 activities. (See Chapter 4 for a more detailed discussion.)

To illustrate this process, consider tying your shoelaces. If you're reading this, you've likely tied a shoelace thousands or even tens of thousands of times. You've been training at shoe tying for so long that you've become an expert. You can literally do it with your eyes closed and without deliberate thought. It's a System 1 task—but this wasn't always the case. When you were young, shoe tying was a complicated System 2 task, requiring much effort and patience on your part (and on your parents' end as well). You had to go carefully through each step of forming a loop with one end of a lace, holding it between your thumb and forefinger, wrapping the other lace around it, and so forth. When you stop to think about it, shoe tying is quite complex. But now that you've put in enough deliberate effort to master it, you can do it naturally via System 1, and it's difficult to do it well using System 2. Try tying your shoe one step at a time while explaining the process to someone. You'll likely need a few tries to get it right, showing that analyzing something you can do automatically is a bad idea. After much practice, your fingers have developed a "muscle memory" for shoe tying, although that term is a misnomer since the memory is not actually stored in your muscles. When we say you have muscle memory, we really mean that the skill has come under the control of System 1, or the autonomic nervous system.

There's a sport psychology trick you can use to take advantage of this process. If you're sparring with someone who's kicking your butt and seems to be "in the zone," ask them to explain in detail exactly what they're doing. This pulls them out of System 1 and into System 2, and if they can't return to the fast-thinking approach, you will have tricked them out of that zone. This is similar to Gallwey's findings in the *Inner Game*, where he encourages learners to stay out of their own way and let the automatic processes do their thing.

One important point: Deliberate practice can make an effortful, complex task become relatively easy, as with shoe tying above. When someone makes a difficult technique look easy—think of a no-look pass in basketball or a series of transitions from one position to another in grappling sports—remember that it took the champion hours and hours of hard work to make it seem effortless.

Of course, there are some downsides to relying too heavily on this approach. One is the risk of making a mindless mistake when something changes. If you've drilled a move over and over, to the point where you do it on autopilot, this will serve you well—until your opponent figures out what you're doing and mounts a new defense. If you're running on automatic, you'll get caught off guard.

One common example from your everyday life is when you encounter road construction on your daily commute. If you drive the same route every day, you probably have had the experience of your car almost "driving itself" to home or work, until you arrive with little memory of the journey. This can work beautifully until a lane is closed unexpectedly—that's when your car may drive itself right into a construction zone. This accounts for a number of accidents and is the reason you often see signs saying "New traffic pattern ahead." Despite the efficiency and expertise that comes with unconscious control, it can sometimes get you into trouble.

System 1 is also subject to bias that often goes undetected. You may believe that System 2 is in control, but your conscious beliefs are informed by your unconscious impressions. For example, you may be getting tired and crave a rest late in a fight, so you decide to take your foot off the gas pedal. This is caused by your primitive instincts kicking in to conserve energy, but in order to rationalize your choice, you convince yourself that you're way ahead on the judges' scorecards and can afford to lose a round. In this type of scenario, it's incredibly difficult to be fully honest with yourself, and it explains why so many competitors are shocked to lose the judges' decision.

Kahneman and Tversky's research supports the longstanding principles of psychoanalytic theory, which asserts that we are often unaware of our unconscious motives and fabricate conscious explanations to justify them. Surround yourself with a team whom you can trust to tell you the truth. Since it's impossible to be honest with yourself all the time, you need to listen to your trusted supporters. (We'll discuss this more in Chapter 12.)

Psyching Up and Settling Down

Notwithstanding the above pitfalls, your autonomic nervous system is exceptionally efficient and fast-thinking. Assuming you're well-trained, it's best to compete without thinking too much. When you trust your training and believe in yourself, it's easy to rely on your instincts. But when you get anxious or take a competition too seriously, you might respond by exerting too much control, veering into System 2, and thinking about things that you would usually do without thinking. You end up "playing tight" and falling into the analysis paralysis trap.

Staying out of that trap is not always easy, although there are a few strategies to follow:

- **Use techniques such as meditation, controlled breathing, and self-talk.** We described the inverted U curve earlier in the book (see Chapter 2), which shows that each of us has an ideal level of arousal. The better you get at moderating your own arousal or anxiety, the more consistently you can perform at your best, and a crucial mechanism behind this is finding the right balance between conscious and unconscious control. Often, when you get anxious, you try to soothe yourself by exerting conscious control over things that are important or could go wrong. The more you learn how to manage your emotions, even in the big competitions—indeed, especially in them—the better you'll master the balance between thinking and not thinking.

- **Allow yourself to be somewhat overhyped leading up to a competition and then transition once the contest begins.** In other words, it's OK to over-think things before you start, but once the whistle blows, let your instincts (i.e., your autonomic nervous system) take over. This strategy works well for athletes who just can't seem to stay calm before a match or a fight. Your mind is all over the place 30 minutes before you're up? No problem. What matters is where your head is when you're actually competing. Knowing this can prevent you from going into a spiral of being anxious about being anxious, which is a dreadful place to be. Anxiety is a lot more tolerable when you look at it as simply part of the process. In effect, the strategy is to use conscious control before a contest, as well as during breaks in the action (such as between rounds). That's when you can be analytical; go time is when you shouldn't think—just do.

- **Focus your desire for conscious control on the appropriate areas.** We've been clear that thinking too much about autonomic processes is a problem, but there are some aspects of the contest that benefit from deliberate thought, such as your timing, your opponent, and the competition area. It's helpful to pay attention to these things.

As an example, in a stand-up fight, you might notice that your opponent tends to circle to the left and dip his head after throwing a combination, so you tell yourself, "The next time he finishes a combination, catch him with my right hand." You're using Kahneman's System 2 to decide *when* to implement your technique but allowing System 1 to handle the actual implementation. Similarly, if you're anxious before a competition and need to direct your nervous mental energy toward something, you can tell yourself, "Make sure you control the center." You'd be "using your head" to consciously direct your attention to where you want your body to be, while "not thinking too much" about what your body is doing. In other words, direct your conscious attention to strategy and let your autonomic nervous system handle the execution.

These principles apply to other performance situations as well, in both sport and non-sport contexts. Paul McBeth, the world champion disc golfer, thinks deliberately about the technique he is going to use as he approaches a shot, accounting for factors such as distance to target, elevation, and wind, but doesn't think during the execution. "Once you step up to actually approach your shot and your routine starts, you shut your head off, and you just let your body go and do everything that you've trained and put hours into," Paul says.

The principle of training extensively so you can act automatically applies in a military context as well. Patrick Regan, a former Navy SEAL (as well as a wrestler and lacrosse player), tells us that thousands of hours go into planning for a specific mission, working with the same team that will be conducting it. In addition, a SEAL's expertise is aided by a debriefing session held after a patrol or mission, known as a "hot wash," so they can learn and improve from it.

As Patrick puts it, "When you dream at night, you should be reflecting on the scenario." This process allows a team to make strategic decisions such as where and when to enter a building and then proceed automatically, based on their many hours of preparation.

Similarly, former Marine and current Sandboxx CEO, pilot, and adventure sport enthusiast Sam Meek says training should get you to a place where you can perform effectively without conscious control. He emphasizes learning and following procedures, training under real-life conditions, and learning from your mistakes as components that allow you to perform seemingly risky tasks automatically. "You have to be incredibly responsible to do what otherwise would be risky things," he says.

Your autonomic and somatic nervous systems are both operating all the time (except during sleep, when your conscious mind is mostly turned off), and you perform at your peak when each system is handling its given tasks. The key is to pay attention to the right things and ignore the rest.

CHAPTER 11

Pushing Through Pain AND Pulling Back On the Reins

Pushing Through Pain

Pros

- Promotes mental toughness/resilience
- Improves mental and physical conditioning
- Allows you to overcome obstacles

Cons

- Can lead to injury and delayed healing
- Can interfere with smart decision making
- Ignores important information from your body

When to Use This Attitude

- When dealing with typical soreness
- To overcome moments of weakness
- During moments requiring high effort

Pulling Back On the Reins

Pros

- Prevents injury
- Promotes healing
- Leads to thoughtful responses to pain

Cons

- Can reduce your resilience
- May prevent full effort
- Can limit your growth and achievement

When to Use This Attitude

- When you are actually injured
- When you're unable to recover normally
- During low-stakes situations, such as youth sports

Pushing Through Pain AND Pulling Back On the Reins: Pros, Cons, and When to Use

"When you win, nothing hurts."

—Joe Namath, former quarterback for the New York Jets
and member of the Pro Football Hall of Fame

At the 2018 NCAA Wrestling Championships, Cornell University's Yianni Diakomihalis suffered a torn ACL in the quarterfinals.

He had a decision to make: He could push through the pain and compete in the semifinals and finals, risking a catastrophic injury to his unstable knee. Or he could prioritize his health and withdraw, denying himself the chance to be a national champion.

"I knew the risks and felt the pain, but that was irrelevant," Yianni says. "So I chose to ignore all that and focus instead on what really mattered, which was wrestling well for the rest of the weekend." And that is what he did, avenging his only prior collegiate loss in the semifinals and then winning the finals in dramatic fashion to become an NCAA champion as a freshman, the first of four he won during his college career.

It's no secret that champions are tough. They don't let struggles or hardships deter them from their goals. They push themselves until it's painful to keep going, and then they keep going nonetheless. They know that success often hurts and they embrace the pain, since it's a sign that they're doing what it takes to win.

Many embrace the notion that pain is weakness leaving the body. In competition, the winner is typically the one who wants it more, and that is often synonymous with tolerating more pain.

At the same time, wise athletes know that pain is also a form of feedback, and they don't completely ignore it. Whether it's muscle fatigue, reaching your cardiovascular maximum, or the pain from an injury, it's often necessary to pull back the reins on yourself, at least in the short term, so you can keep going in the long term. You slow down so you don't need to stop.

So when should you push through the pain, and when is it best to pull back? First, it's important to know yourself, so you can see on which side of the equation you tend to fall. If you're like many dedicated competitors, you'd rather pass out from pain than quit. You'd let someone break your arm before tapping out. If this is you, you'd be well-served to pull back on the reins a bit more. Although this toughness can be admirable, it can also lead to easily avoidable injuries. If you value toughness above all else, you risk making poor decisions in the name of pushing through pain, which is a form of tough-stupid behavior (see Figure 2.3 on page 31). University of Pittsburgh wrestling coach Keith Gavin and Ben, along with many other coaches, have observed these tendencies among athletes whose highly competitive nature leads them to take unnecessary risks even in the practice room. The wise coach promotes this toughness, but also advocates for more intelligent decision making.

If you tend to get injured a lot (especially if you've been diagnosed with an overuse injury), you likely need to listen to your body more than you currently do. If you think that constitutes wimping out, we can assure you that you don't need to keep proving how tough you are. Focus instead on becoming more intelligent—and tough.

But if you have a history of injury defaults and visits to a trainer or doctor, only to be told that you're not actually injured, work on increasing your pain tolerance and pushing through it. You may be assuming that pain always means you're injured, but sometimes it's a natural part of training and competition. Learn to distinguish pain from real injury.

Knowing your tendencies in relating to pain is useful, and having others help you with your strategy is better still. If you have coaches and trainers who know you well, they can be invaluable in helping you decide when to push through or pull back. If they know you'll pass out from pain before complaining, they can tell you to take it easy or go get your nagging injury checked out, and you ought to listen to them. On the flip side, if they feel you need to toughen up or are still anxious about a prior injury that has healed, they can push you.

MMA fighter Chris Weidman describes his communication with his coach, Ray Longo, around the various injuries he's faced. "He knows I'm going to try to kill myself every single day," Chris says. "So if I'm seriously hurt, he doesn't want to make it worse. He just wants to get me in there as healthy as possible." This is in contrast to needing a coach to "call your bluff," as Chris phrases it, if you're being too cautious.

It's also critical to seek professional advice. Some injuries cause nagging pain, but won't get worse with exertion, while others can go from a minor issue to a major problem if you ignore them. A sore shoulder or knee, for example, might hurt more after a hard practice but not be at risk of further injury, but a slight tear in the cartilage around your rib could heal well with rest but get much worse with further strain. Most athletes and coaches don't have the expertise to offer sound guidance, so it's essential to heed the advice of medical personnel, ideally ones with special training in sports medicine.

Concussions deserve particular attention. They carry symptoms beyond pain, such as confusion and impaired memory, and there is long-term risk in ignoring them. And because the culture of sport typically favors pushing through rather than pulling back, many sport governing bodies have established strict protocols for return to play, which rely on the opinions of medical personnel.

Dr. Anna Lembke, the medical director of the Stanford Addiction Medicine clinic and author of the excellent book *Dopamine Nation* (among other publications), distinguishes between "good pain" and "bad pain."

Good pain: "The pain that comes from pushing the body to the limit of what it can endure and is naturally striving to achieve."

Bad pain: "When our body is signaling to us that damage is being done, that the activity is going beyond what that particular body was designed to do." She explains that this bad, injurious pain is often sharp, acute, or localized. In addition, Dr. Lembke says, athletes cross over into the bad pain area when they experience excessive fatigue that doesn't rebound with rest: "You have to treat your body as a sacred instrument and have a healthy respect for what your body is telling you."

So, for example, you can pursue good pain by pushing yourself so hard that you run out of oxygen and force your body to go anaerobic in the final stretch of a workout, or bad pain by denying yourself fluids and experiencing dehydration—with no weigh-in in sight.

In *Dopamine Nation*, Dr. Lembke writes extensively about the body's natural tendency to seek a balance between pleasure and pain, which is mitigated by the neurotransmitter dopamine. Problems occur when you lean too far in one direction or the other. While too much pain can be damaging, not enough pain is a problem, too. She references the Greek concept of hormesis, which literally means "to set in motion."

Dr. Lembke explains, "Hormesis is the science of using just the right amount of pain to set into motion the body's own ability to become strong. The idea is to use pain as a triggering event to incite the body's natural healing mechanisms." Thus, when coaches and athletes advocate for enduring pain to make us stronger, the science checks out. According to Dr. Lembke, "When you experience the optimal amount of pain, you are creating a powerful, self-propelling cascade, in your own body, to realize its most amazing, awe-inspiring potential."

When to Push Through and Pull Back

Another consideration in pushing through or pulling back: the stage you're in during your season or a specific competition. If you're feeling the pain of exertion early in a contest and ignore it, you're apt to be exhausted before the end and unable to push through. Many athletes needlessly die on their swords this way. It would be better to shift into a lower gear and exert yourself more judiciously throughout the competition. This is part and parcel of endurance sports such as long-distance running, triathlons, and Spartan Races. Many novices incorrectly assume that the best racers are the ones who ignore or push through their pain and fatigue. Although elite endurance athletes do possess extreme mental toughness, they are also skilled at listening to their bodies.

The physical signals of pain and fatigue are essential feedback for making intelligent and strategic decisions throughout a race. Ignoring them would be the equivalent of operating a machine with a broken thermostat. It will eventually overheat. Skilled runners who get close to "hitting the wall" with miles to go will likely pull back. If they're in the final stretch of the race, however, they'll push through and start their sprint.

Valent Sinković, the champion rower, tells us that early in his career, he experienced "going over the edge too soon" and becoming drained. "I wanted to help the team to go faster, and I overdid it sometimes," he says. Valent and his brother Martin have both become more proficient at maintaining an ideal pace by targeting this facet of competition during their training sessions. Like any other skill, finding the balance between pushing through and pulling back is achieved through deliberate practice.

Effective decision making in this area requires you to consider your level of fatigue, your opponent's energy level, your fitness, and the time remaining in the contest. Going hard and exhausting your opponent can be an effective strategy if you're in better shape, but it is naïve and simplistic to assume it's best to go all out all the time. Indeed, having only one speed is a liability when you're up against a skilled opponent—it makes you predictable. Just as a pitcher who throws only fastballs rarely succeeds against skilled batters, combatants rarely triumph at the highest levels unless they mix up the pace.

Just as you respond to fatigue differently at various points in a competition, how you handle an injury depends on the timing as well. If you tweak your knee early in a contest, it may be a good idea to take a default, depending on the possible severity and the importance of the event. If it's an early season matchup in college, and your individual win or loss won't affect the team outcome, it would be foolish to risk further damage and jeopardize your whole season. If it's the national finals, though, you might opt to push through the pain, even at risk of further injury, because it means so much to you. Here again, it helps to have others around you to help with the decision, which you sometimes have to make quickly and under great pressure.

If your injury occurs prior to a competition, you face the same issues, but you have more time to make a thoughtful decision. We talked about Ben's rib injury in Chapter 9, which he sustained three weeks before the NCAA championships. Ben could have pushed through the pain and kept training as planned, but this would have exacerbated the injury. So he made the difficult decision to limit his sparring and hard drilling, sacrificing match-level fitness to be as healthy as possible, and he made this tough-smart decision after talking to trusted members of his support network.

Another variable to consider in deciding whether to push through or pull back is your current level of competition. Listen up, youth coaches and parents: Young athletes at this level do not need to push through injuries. Sure, you may hope they will gain some toughness through their sport, but at the youth level, safety is a higher priority. At the very least, coaches and parents need to use caution when encouraging a young child to endure the pain of an injury. As kids mature and become more committed to their sport, then they can be pushed, and push themselves through pain, a bit harder.

An associated concern in youth sports is the risk of overuse injuries. Well-established findings show that kids who specialize in a single sport at a young age are far more likely to develop an overuse injury compared to those who participate in a variety of activities. These injuries are especially common in sports that involve repetitive motions that strain a child's developing bones and joints, such as pitching in baseball. So when a young athlete develops nagging joint pain (with knee, shoulder, and elbow injuries typically topping the list), the research suggests they ought to take a break, not push through it.

Though popular belief holds that to be great, kids need to commit to one sport at a young age, the vast majority of eventual champions go through a "sampling phase," where they participate in a variety of sports and other activities before deciding to focus on one. Research by Benjamin Bloom and his colleagues in the 1980s, published in the seminal book *Developing Talent in Young People*, and by Jean Côté and associates in the 1990s and 2000s, has shown for decades that achieving expertise is a developmental process. It's best to delay specialization until adolescence, when kids' bodies (and minds) have matured a bit more. Children are not simply smaller versions of adults, and they should not be expected to respond to pain and struggle the same way a college or professional athlete would. At a young age, kids need to be allowed to pull back on the reins and then learn to push through the pain as they develop and grow.

Pain as a Psychological Experience

We often think of pain as a physical experience, but it has some very strong psychological components as well (that's without addressing whether it's even possible to separate the physical from the psychological). Psychologists and neuroscientists regard pain as a multifaceted phenomenon. One common distinction is between *pain threshold* and *pain tolerance.*

Pain threshold is the point at which a person recognizes a sensation as painful. Some fighters can absorb a solid blow and honestly say, "That didn't hurt." They have a high pain threshold. Others feel the pain of every punch or kick, exhibiting a lower pain threshold. Yet this does not imply that those with a low pain threshold are less likely to push through it.

Rather, one's ability to endure the pain once it is felt is known as pain tolerance. When we talk about mental toughness, we're typically referring to your pain tolerance. If you have a low pain tolerance, you're likely to submit to the pain once you hit your pain threshold, whether that threshold is high or low. In other words, as soon as you feel pain, you quit. If you have a high pain tolerance, you can feel pain and persevere nonetheless.

Let's look again at endurance sports: A competitor running with no attention at all to their pain or fatigue (i.e., with a "broken thermostat") would be demonstrating a high pain threshold, but that can actually be damaging to their strategy. In contrast, those who are in sync with their bodies have a lower pain threshold but a high pain tolerance, so they can push through when needed. In endurance sports and others where fatigue is a factor, an ideal way to compete is with a low to moderate pain threshold, so you can use pain as feedback about your body's condition, as well as a relatively high pain tolerance so you have the option to keep going when you have to.

We experience pain for a reason: It helps us survive by telling us what to avoid. Yet pain is not inherently bad. As most athletes know, you need to endure some pain if you want to improve—and sometimes survive. In 2021, on the *Wrestling Changed My Life* podcast, former wrestler Jay Jackson told host Ryan Warner about an incident when he was held hostage at gunpoint by a stalker. Blindfolded, his ankles and wrists bound, and in pain, Jay recalled training with a particularly tough workout partner, Mike Shmidlin, who used pain strategically as a weapon in the wrestling room. Having built a high pain tolerance through many workouts with Mike, Jay was prepared to endure the pain when his life was at risk, and he was able to fight back and overcome his captor.

Our experience of pain—in both threshold and tolerance—is influenced by a variety of psychological factors, as well as physical ones. Think of a child with a big test for which they are unprepared.

They are much more likely to get a stomachache and ask to go home than on a day when they have studied and feel ready for the exam. Among adults, the connection between job satisfaction and health is so well-established that the number of employee sick days being used is often tracked as a major indicator of job satisfaction—or the lack of it.

Athletes also experience pain differently, depending on our overall performance. This influence is present acutely during a competition and more generally throughout the year. When you're winning a match or confident that you can win, you're more likely to shrug off even excruciating pain. But if you're tired or don't believe you can pull out the victory, you're more likely to experience any pain as intolerable. We've all seen athletes sustain injuries as a face-saving way to explain why they got their butt kicked. Of course, the more you train hard and endure pain in the process, the more psychological strength you build, alongside the gains you make in your physical and technical skills.

Just as your acute situation in competition influences how you experience and respond to pain, so does your long-term mental state. When you're feeling good psychologically, the little bumps and bruises you get along the way don't bother you much. But when you're feeling stressed and burned out, being injured can start to look appealing. Perhaps you would never skip a practice because you're tired, stressed, or in a bad mood, but a bum knee would give you a solid excuse to take some days off (or, on particularly bad days, even retire from your sport). You might even start doing risky things to raise the odds of getting hurt. This phenomenon of having an injury serve as cover for a hidden desire to quit has been referred to as an "honorable discharge" from sport.

It is important to distinguish physical symptoms that have a full or partial psychological cause from someone who is faking an injury, which is known as *malingering*. Most athletes experiencing pain that can't be explained medically are not faking it—their psychological issues are likely being expressed in a physical manner. In mental health jargon, these situations fall under the umbrella of somatic disorders, which boils down to a person's body communicating a message that they are unwilling or unable to say. For example, if an athlete has partial paralysis in one arm and all available medical and neurological tests can't identify a cause, the explanation might be that the athlete, in whole or in part, doesn't want to compete. Often, this desire is an unconscious one—that's why it's expressed by their body rather than through words.

Many athletes who develop somatic disorders don't do it because they're mentally weak—they do it because they're mentally tough. Most people's minds break down before their bodies do, so they respond by reducing their effort or taking a break. But some people are so mentally tough—or stubborn, if you will— that they keep pushing until their body puts a stop to it. When an athlete experiences a somatic sabotage of this kind, they may not need conventional medical treatment, but working with a sport psychologist can be helpful.

Whether you turn to a sport psychologist, physician, athletic trainer, or strength and conditioning coach, these trained professionals can offer helpful guidance as part of your support network. And having a solid support network or being part of a team is critical in making tough, wise decisions when it comes to pushing yourself—or pulling back.

CHAPTER 12

Being an Individual AND Being a Team Player

Being an Individual

Pros

- Focuses on your needs and goals
- Promotes self-reliance
- Prevents others taking advantage of you

Cons

- Can alienate others
- May limit the support you receive
- Limits learning and development

When to Use This Attitude

- During individual competition
- When pursuing challenging goals
- When not working on shared tasks

Being a Team Player

Pros

- Fosters mutually supportive relationships
- Promotes camaraderie
- Leads to seeking help effectively

Cons

- Can lead to deferring your needs
- May reduce independence
- May take on burdens of others

When to Use This Attitude

- When working toward shared goals
- When among good, supportive people
- When you and/or others need help

Being an Individual AND Being a Team Player: Pros, Cons, and When to Use

"The best for the group comes when everyone in the group does what's best for himself and the group."

—John Nash, Nobel Prize-winning mathematician

"When you're out there on the mat with another guy who's quicker and faster than you, there's not a whole hell of a lot a team can do for you."

—Louden Swain (played by actor Matthew Modine), *Vision Quest*

Anyone who has competed in an individual sport will tell you nothing compares to succeeding on your own. The corollary, though, is that the pain of losing, with no one to blame but yourself, cuts deep. Being out there on your own teaches you to be self-reliant and develop a rugged sense of independence.

Yet athletes who succeed in these sports are often the greatest team players you'll find. Team camaraderie is a highly underrated aspect of solo sports. The assumption is that these athletes only focus on themselves, but there is no better incentive to support one another than the shared experience of being on your own against a hostile opponent. There's a strong incentive to help each other out and pull for one another in the individual battles. In this way, you can strive to be both an individual and a team player.

There are times it helps to be selfish and other times when generosity is the way to go. We have seen athletes err on both sides. Some are so focused on their goals that their sole reason for interacting with others is to use them. This approach can work, but it can get you only so far. Staying self-focused ensures you'll devote time and energy only to those things that move you toward your goals, but others are likely to tire of their role as your supporters, especially if you don't reciprocate. Failing to foster mutually beneficial relationships eventually ends in no relationships, and in the long term it's impossible to succeed on your own.

On the other hand, athletes who focus too heavily on being a good teammate sometimes end up deferring their own goals and success in service to others. This can take many forms, including letting your partner work on their technique without taking time to work on your own, allowing others to take up your coach's time so that you miss out on individual attention, and generally getting pushed to the side due to not wanting to appear selfish.

If you find yourself frustrated by giving more to others than you're getting in return, that's a sign that you'd benefit from being more selfish. We explained in Chapter 2 that people run into problems when they value a principle so much that they pathologize its opposite, which is often true with overly generous people. It's wonderful to be generous, but if you think that withholding charity makes you selfish, your aversion to being selfish will make you a doormat. If you are being walked over, it's time to focus on your own needs.

The opposite is true as well. If you're focused only on what's best for you, you're likely to become more and more isolated. So if you're finding it hard to get people to train with you, work on being a better teammate and give some attention to others' needs.

MMA fighter Gerald Meerschaert says that as a featured athlete, it's tempting to believe everyone is looking out for your best interest, but this is often not the case. "Finding out that you're not that important to others and that you need to look out for yourself—that will go a long way for a lot of people," he says.

NFL veteran Chase Coffman describes several dilemmas he faced as a team-sport athlete when deciding whether to push through injuries. Some team personnel urged him to push through and risk it in service to the team, while others encouraged him to consider what was best for his long-term well-being as an individual. Chase describes this as a constant balance, concluding, "Ultimately, you have to make those decisions for yourself. Nobody can make them for you."

Finding Win-Win Relationships

Finding a balance between fulfilling your needs and others' needs often becomes a moot point when you're surrounded by good people—the ones who leave you feeling better and more energized when you interact with them. The wrong ones leave you feeling drained.

Mark Ellis, the heavyweight wrestling champion, distinguishes between "life givers" and "life-takers" and describes the negativity he found among some fellow athletes early in his college career: "When I was thinking about not wrestling and spoke with other people who complained and said, 'It's not fair,' I felt worse," he explains. "Then when I got around people who said, 'You can do this, you're good enough, you can be a champion,' then that was something I started to believe."

When you surround yourself with life-givers, as Mark puts it, their influence on you (and vice versa) is mutually beneficial. Devoting energy to them serves you as well, and what's best for you is also what's best for your team. But if you find yourself expending energy helping others without getting a return on that investment, focus on what's best for you and seek out others who have your best interests in mind.

Chase describes having a similar philosophy as a team member. He played as a tight end, a position in football that is sometimes a receiving target (with associated statistics and accolades) and at other times tasked with the less glorified role of blocker. "The success of the team ultimately drives the success or opportunity for yourself," he says. He adds that the best coaches and general managers recognize that the team's success is the product of each individual doing their job on each play, so they seek athletes who are devoted team players and can be counted on regardless of their individual achievements. The ideal team environment, according to Chase, is when players have the attitude, "It doesn't matter [who is getting the touches]. We're all winning." As the saying goes, a rising tide lifts all boats.

The guiding principle has been labeled as "Think Win-Win," which is the fourth of the "seven habits of highly effective people" originally outlined by Stephen Covey in his 1989 book. The wisdom of thinking win-win means that you seek out partnerships that benefit both you and the other party. If it's a loss for you and a win for them, that's a no-go, but if it's a win for you and a loss for them, that's a no-go as well in terms of working together. (Of course, in competition, you're looking to win while handing your opponent a loss.) Only when the relationship is mutually beneficial should you pursue it. This principle can guide not only your sport-related connections but also your relationships in all aspects of life.

When you pursue win-win solutions, wonderful synergies can emerge. The "funky" style of wrestling that Ben established grew out of his need to find a solution to a potential win-lose situation.

As a young wrestler, Ben was more enthusiastic about the sport than any of his friends or teammates, and he became significantly better than they were. He needed workout partners, but if he simply beat up on them every day, they wouldn't come back, or if they did, they'd be demoralized. They needed to get something out of it as well. Ben's solution was to let his partners get close to scoring on him. He would then come up with funky techniques to defend against the takedowns they were almost completing. His partners got to feel the excitement and confidence that came from almost scoring, and Ben got to develop the creative, funky style that became a hallmark of his wrestling career.

One common win-win situation occurs when you're trying to improve at your craft and are asked to teach someone else. There's a phenomenon new coaches often experience in which teaching others has a strong positive impact on their own performance. Without even thinking about it, they find that their own execution becomes smoother and crisper after teaching techniques to others. Explaining a skill requires you to think about it in deeper and more nuanced ways than you would otherwise need to do. To be an effective teacher, you must develop a more comprehensive understanding of the subject yourself.

This principle is well-understood by educators in various fields, including medical education, where the "see one, do one, teach one" approach is common. First you watch someone else demonstrate the skill. Then you do it yourself. Then you teach someone else how to do it, which brings you to the highest level of understanding and accelerates you toward expertise.

So when a teammate asks you to show them how to do that technique you do so well, by obliging them, you'll help them improve, but you'll also get better in the process. If you have a benevolent spirit, you'll also feel good about being helpful. And if you, in turn, ask them to show you one of their best techniques, you'll both benefit further, with the learner and teacher roles reversed. By giving help, you help yourself, and vice versa.

Giving and Receiving Help

Sometimes it's better to give, and other times it's better to receive. In some situations, these transitions occur rather quickly. For example, in a drill session or sparring session, athletes take turns working on their own and then being a good partner. The partners may switch roles every minute or so, or even every few seconds. This typically occurs when both are actively preparing for competition. Many athletes neglect the *good partner* part, which is a skill in its own right, requiring you to give the right amount of resistance and adopt an active teacher mentality. It's important to develop these skills and put them into practice when your job is to help your partner get better.

In other situations, you may be in the role of receiving help rather than giving it for an extended period of time. For example, if you've made an Olympic team or you're preparing for a championship fight, your success becomes the focus of your team of supporters. In 2020, American wrestling legend John Smith described this type of self-focused period to *Wrestling Changed My Life* podcast host Ryan Warner, discussing his mentality following a loss to the Cuban wrestler Lazaro Reinoso.

"My time, I got real stingy with it after that loss," he says. When asked about prioritizing world and Olympic titles, John adds, "It's a self-centered world. It can be a selfish world." John's friend and mentor Dave "Doc" Bennett explains, "When you're in the process of trying to win championships . . . if you're not focused on yourself and what your needs are and what you need to do to win that, I think you're making a mistake." He adds, "There's a time to be selfish and a time to pay back, and the time to pay back is when the journey is over, when you have time to dedicate yourself to doing that in the proper fashion." If you're seeking to balance out how much you take vs. how much you give, you will run a surplus at times and a deficit at others, depending on the stage of your season and career.

It's OK to say no to others' requests. It's also OK—and necessary—to accept help from others. You don't have to pay them back, at least not immediately. If they are freely offering to help you, they're getting something out of it already, whether it's the warm feeling of being helpful or the chance to give back after having received help themselves. If you feel an obligation to your willing supporters, you can fulfill it by expressing gratitude—a valuable return on investment for those who invest in you.

If you're hesitant to ask for help, know that even the most rugged individualists seek out support from others. If you resist, you're limiting your own growth and improvement.

This happens in weight rooms every day. When someone is looking to "max out" on the bench press or squat rack, they seek out a "spotter," not because they're admitting weakness, but because they're looking to enhance their strength. With a helper-spotter, they can push themselves in ways that would be unsafe on their own. In turn, the spotter doesn't do the work for them, but assists them in their training. A good spotter won't take the bar at the first sign of trouble, but offer encouragement to push through the pain of exertion to complete the lift on their own.

In the weight room and elsewhere, we encourage you to ask for help, not to take the easy way out but to enhance your progress. It would be foolish to prioritize self-reliance at all times. Many devoted athletes would agree that using a spotter makes good sense. Most would also support getting help from a coach for technical and strategic advice. Yet they recoil from asking for help when it omes to personal or emotional struggles. This is misguided. If your goal is to be the best you can be, then you should be receptive to help in any form that can make you better.

Dan Gable, known as a beacon of mental toughness, is a strong advocate of "going for help," as he phrases it, as a guiding principle. "Use people's expertise, if better than you or if you don't have the time to do it really well," he says. "There is no need to reinvent the wheel when the wheel is already invented."

Helping Yourself

When it comes to seeking help from others, it's common for athletes to err on the side of not doing enough. Nonetheless, there are occasions when you need to be self-reliant. For the individual sport athlete, the clearest of these is during competition, when nobody can help you but yourself. A coach or cornerman can offer guidance and give you motivation, but ultimately no one but you can complete the task at hand.

There are other times when a coach or training partner will be unavailable and you'll need to figure things out on your own. If you find yourself running for help at the first sign of trouble, you likely need to put more energy and effort into becoming self-reliant. If this is true of you, you're probably receiving corrective feedback from others, telling you to try a bit more on your own first. Often, the greatest leaps in your game come from the self-discovery process.

Becoming a self-regulated learner (i.e., someone who can coach yourself through things) is invaluable. In essence, you should aim to be both coachable and self-reliant. In competitive tennis, coaching is generally not allowed, and being able to self-regulate on the court is essential. Megan Moulton-Levy, of the USTA and Junior Champions Tennis Center, talks about "coaching myself out of a job." She says, "A lot of players look so much to their coaches to tell them what to do that it doesn't serve them well when they're competing. As a coach, you've got to get that person to where they understand what they're doing and be able to do it without you." It is important to be receptive to coaching and other forms of help, but it is equally important to be self-reliant when needed.

For many athletes, even as they're competing alone, their awareness of the supportive team behind them—and their appreciation for that team—is a source of inspiration and motivation. Nick Garone, an All-American wrestler for Old Dominion University in 1991, discussed this concept on the *Wrestling Changed My Life* podcast in 2021. "You always want to win for yourself," Nick says. "But when you want to win for a coach, that takes your game to a whole other level. You feel like you've got an extra two-point lead, because you've got those guys in your corner. It's an incredible feeling."

Other athletes, however, perceive their coaches and supporters as a source of pressure and anxiety. Sometimes this is due to trouble in the coach-athlete relationship, and other times it's caused by the athlete's social anxiety. If you feel adversely impacted by your support team, focus on being an individual when you're out there in the fight. This can take the pressure off and help you compete unburdened. Megan recalls adopting this mentality when her support network became a source of pressure on the tennis court. "I felt a lot of gratitude for all the support," she says. "But when people's expectations got out of whack, I'd push back and focus on myself, since I'm the one out there having to manage myself and perform under these conditions."

Megan also describes the benefit of internalizing the support she received from others and channeling their voices in her self-talk. "I think the best tennis players can also be their own coach or own teammate," she explains. "They can pop in and out between being the individual who has to perform and also being the person who can be positive, be supportive, be demanding, be loving, be stern." In short, she says, "When you think about the benefits of being on a team, the best players can also provide that for themselves."

Team Players In and Out of the Gym

A final consideration in being both an individual and a team player is the difference between working toward shared goals with your team members and bonding with them on a social level. Social psychologists draw a distinction between "task cohesion" and "social cohesion." Task cohesion is the binding force that group members experience while working toward a common goal. Any dissonance among athletes, or between athletes and their coaches and support staff, becomes a threat to achieving that goal. In this context, it is important to work well together.

In contrast, social cohesion refers to the sense of connectedness group members feel on a social level. Essentially, if a team has high social cohesion, they like to hang out together in their free time. While this can be nice and often makes working together more enjoyable, it is not necessary for a team to function effectively.

Many coaches seek to build a "family atmosphere," and many athletes are drawn to this, but as long as a team possesses mutual respect and its members support one another in pursuing their goals, social cohesion is not essential. In fact, it is important for coaches and athletes not to allow their social affinity (or the lack of it) to affect their rational decision making about issues such as who makes the starting lineup or whom to choose as a sparring partner. Base those decisions on who is the best person for the job. When working toward shared goals, it's important to be a good team player, but when it comes to socializing, it's fine to be an individual.

The distinction between task and social cohesion highlights that the "right" way to be within sports and competitions does not necessarily generalize to non-sport domains. However, there are aspects of sport and combat that do provide wonderful lessons for your life in general. We'll discuss those in our final chapter.

Sport as Preparation for Life, Except When It's Not

"Sports do not build character; they reveal it."

—Heywood Hale Broun, CBS sports commentator

"Sports don't build character; they build characters."

—Unknown

One of the favorite pastimes of old athletes and coaches is waxing poetic about how wonderfully their chosen sport prepares an athlete for life. "It's about much more than fighting/boxing/wrestling/MMA/karate/tennis/etc.," they say. "It's about learning discipline, overcoming obstacles, and realizing you're capable of more than you thought." And these are only a few of the many "life lessons" that sport can teach, they claim. Take them at their word, and these ancient warriors will convince you that participating in their sport is a surefire way of ensuring a successful and happy life.

Indeed, many accomplished professionals attribute their success to lessons learned through sport. But there are many other people—less likely to be quoted in the media—who competed valiantly in sport and later became downtrodden or even incarcerated.

This is not to deny that sport offers valuable life lessons. They certainly do, and sport is often an excellent metaphor for life in general. But some lessons translate poorly, or even in harmful ways. In this final chapter, we'll look at several ways in which sport does and does not set you up for success in life—and the times when it's helpful or harmful to use your sport as a guide for your non-sport actions and decisions. We'll also offer some guidance on situations when athletes would and would not benefit from viewing their sport as a way to develop character and gain life lessons.

What We Learn from Sport

We could devote an entire book to the ways in which positive qualities can be developed through sport; many volumes have already been written about it. We have mentioned Ryan Warner's *Wrestling Changed My Life* podcast several times; as the title implies, it is devoted to the concept. In the opening sequence of each episode, various wrestlers describe what the sport teaches, including adaptability, endurance, self-reflection, resilience, picking yourself up after failing, humility, and mental toughness. Ask any devoted athlete from any sport, and they will eagerly tell you how their sport has positively influenced them in life.

One such athlete is Jurica Barac. Jure (as he is called by his friends) is a former professional BMX rider and Red Bull athlete and current CEO of Highlander, the world's leading long-distance hiking adventure company. When asked how his sport experience helps him in business, Jure recalls the painstaking process of learning a difficult skill, such as a front flip on a BMX bike. Perfecting it can require a full month or more of repeating the technique on a safe surface as many times as necessary, until he has succeeded dozens of times in a row. Only then does the rider perform the technique in an actual BMX venue.

"The practice gives you the confidence," Jure says. "I learned that I can do extremely difficult things if I put in the time and effort." He explains that the self-confidence gained through sport has removed any doubts about his ability to complete a challenging task or close a deal for his company. He knows that success is not limited by his ability but rather by his will. "Business is now about whether I want to do it," he says.

In this sense, BMX riding is a useful metaphor for business, but in other ways, the extreme sport and business worlds are quite different. As a reminder of these differences, Jure keeps a photo in his office of him completing a front flip in competition for the first time. Performing this skill carries a very real risk of major injuries such as paralysis, or even death. Business has financial and other risks, of course, but no direct risk to your physical well-being. Jure explains, "Whenever I start to get stressed in business, I look at that picture of the front flip, and it reminds me that I'm not going to die in business, so there's nothing to worry about." After enduring the struggles of sport, other things become a bit easier.

Those struggles can help us learn humility and empathy as well. Speaking with Joe De Sena on *The Hard Way* podcast in 2021, Ilias Diakomihalis, a former All-American wrestler and father to several outstanding athletes, says, "Suffering creates humility, which allows you to empathize with others, because you feel it. By putting yourself in situations when you're stripped raw, you can associate with others [who are suffering]." Ilias adds, "Our lives can get pretty easy, and we can get full of ourselves and detached from reality. The more you create humility in your own life, the more you become a better person and a more functional person."

Tiffany Smiley attributes much of her success to lessons learned through sport. As a triage nurse and military spouse, Tiffany defied the U.S. government's directive to sign discharge papers for her husband, Scotty, after he was wounded and permanently blinded while serving in Iraq. The story of how Scotty became America's first blind active-duty army officer is told in his book *Hope Unseen*. According to Tiffany, "Playing competitive high school and collegiate sports, especially as a girl, really added a ton of value to my life." She especially highlights the grit and perseverance developed through sport, telling us, "Those factors, walking into that hospital room, were the backbone behind me in having that strength to face my fears head-on."

Tiffany also notes that, in some domains, the grit and assertiveness you earn through sport are not exactly welcomed. "As a young adult, you're no longer on that soccer field, having that outlet for your aggression and your confidence, so trying to navigate and channel that in the world is a little bit more delicate of a process," she says. "That competitive, confident, aggressive nature is good. It just can get misperceived, especially in females, when it's not on a sports field."

Still, Tiffany strongly promotes the positive transfer of sport-related lessons to other activities, including her current endeavors as a public servant. "Not being afraid to fail was a huge part of my upbringing," she says, "and now, going into politics, I'll do everything in my power to win, but I'm not afraid of losing." She adds, "Some people won't put themselves out there because they might lose, and I don't think life is lived to the fullest if you're living with that mindset."

When Sport Does Not Prepare You for Life

Given all the ways sport can make us better people, you may be tempted to believe that all its lessons can be applied to non-sport endeavors as a recipe for success. This conclusion would be faulty, though, as there are significant differences between sports and other areas of life. For one, sport competitions are a zero-sum game. When two competitors engage, they may both benefit in some ways from the experience, but if one wins, the other must lose, for a sum of zero. This is not the case in many non-sport settings. For example, when romantic partners fight, it's best for them to look for "win-win" resolutions. In business agreements, prudent collaborators seek opportunities where all parties reap greater profits.

In 2021, lacrosse legend Paul Rabil described the competitive attitude that made him so successful as an athlete to host Shane Parrish on *The Knowledge Project* podcast. Rabil says, "A competitive asshole is what you have to become, in sports at least." He goes on to contrast sports with business or life. "What I've learned in business and in life is you've got to be a competitive compromiser," he says. "And that requires kindness, empathy, [and] ingenuity."

Indeed, for a business collaboration to succeed in the long term, all parties need to benefit. This is true for personal relationships as well, including friendships and romantic partnerships. It can be difficult for a competitor, who is accustomed to fighting for the win, to engage in collaborative problem solving with a partner. A conflict or disagreement is likely to trigger that old competitive drive, spurring you to try to "win" the argument. But for you to win it, your partner has to lose, and that kind of zero-sum approach does not help the relationship. You'd be better off seeking a compromise in the form of mutual understanding and collaborative resolution.

The competitive fire you learned in sport can at times transfer to life in a harmful way—but that doesn't mean you need to abandon the useful lessons you gained there. As you work through relationship troubles in a collaborative manner, you will benefit by using your sport-informed understanding that success requires sustained effort over time. The value of hard work remains the same, as does the knowledge that most things worth having require it. Whether you're facing a tough opponent in the ring, managing a business through an economic downturn, or working through challenges in a relationship, your ability to keep at it rather than quitting remains a valuable quality.

Another aspect of life that is not well-served by the typical athlete-combatant mindset is leisure or recreation. Sport is achievement oriented, so it translates quite well to fields such as academics or business and wealth accumulation. But it can have negative effects on recreational activities such as socializing, relaxing, and going on vacation. Turning a vacation into a competition can defeat the purpose. If you, like many athletes, want to be the very best in whatever you do, it can help to ask yourself if an activity is an achievement-oriented one. Is it something at which you can improve? Will getting "better" at it serve any useful purpose? If the answer to these questions is yes, then go ahead and work your butt off to achieve your goals. If the answer is no, then take a few deep breaths and focus on enjoying yourself. Not everything is a competition.

When to Leverage and When to Avoid
the "Sport = Life" Mentality

Just as there are times you should leverage your sport-related lessons and times you should refrain, there are also moments as an athlete when it's helpful to view your sport as life preparation and times when it's better to focus on the sport itself. Many parents and youth coaches emphasize that children are learning valuable life lessons along with the techniques and rules of the game, which can help motivate young athletes and encourage them to participate. It can also backfire—especially when adults assert that children's behavior in a sport indicates how they will conduct themselves in life. That creates an exceptionally high-stakes situation for the young people.

Consider a young grappler fighting through nerves while also struggling against a submission attempt. If they see it as an opportunity to demonstrate that they can endure pain and fatigue to overcome life's obstacles, it could provide greater incentive, if they have sufficient maturity and confidence. But if they fail, they will be revealing to their parents and coaches that they are not resilient and are bound to be a disappointment in life. This is why it's generally better to focus on fun and learning at the youth sport level, so that an athlete's decision to tap out or not is due to their present skill level or momentary fatigue rather than an indicator of their core character traits.

Even Sigmund Freud, who showed how our actions reveal our deepest drives, is believed to have said, "Sometimes a cigar is just a cigar."

Among older competitors, emphasizing sport-life connections is more warranted, at least sometimes. This is especially true when your motivation is waning and you are beginning to wonder, "Why am I doing this?" When the sport itself doesn't provide incentive to persevere, reminding yourself that the journey will yield results down the road can provide that extra boost to push through the tough times.

In contrast, when you're already feeling the weight of the world on your shoulders as an athlete, you need no further encouragement to up the ante. In those times, it's better to think of it as just a game (or fight, as the case may be). No need to prove to yourself that you have what it takes to succeed in life. Just go out there, focus on the task at hand, compete hard, and enjoy yourself.

The Path to Extreme Balance

As you can probably tell by this point, we're not big believers in quick-fix, secret-trick advice that makes you believe you can achieve your goals in a snap. Just like physical training and development, growing and adapting to an Extreme Balance mindset also takes time, training, coaching, and hard work.

That said, we can guide you to take some steps toward a winning mentality that will support and enhance your physical skills. Ideally, you'll work closely with coaches, teammates, and others who can help you think about the paradoxes we've highlighted throughout this book. Ultimately, though, it comes down to *you*:

- How honest you are with yourself
- How willing you are to think, imagine, and open yourself up to new ideas
- How you approach the concept of Extreme Balance

The 10,000-hour/10-year principle of skill mastery that we discussed in Chapter 4 applies to mental training as well, so understand that Extreme Balance requires a commitment that no magic-bullet mantras can eliminate. But first, you can equip yourself with the tools that will help you get there. We recommend you start with the following five areas:

1. **Read**: Sometimes you can get so wrapped up in your own life and in training that you don't take the time to learn about what others have done to become elite. Read biographies of champions (in all areas of life, not just sports), as well as other books that have life lessons about performance. When you read, look for the connections: What lessons can you draw from to improve your training and approach to competition? Ben runs a book club with the athletes he trains, to give them potential paths to pursue, and they discuss key moments and concepts together. Reading and discussing what you've read with others is a great way to expand your perspective.

2. **Receive**: Receive feedback, that is. Of course, you're used to getting all kinds of feedback from coaches, but what happens if you expand your circle of trust? Ask a friend or training partner for candid feedback, not just about your tactics, but also about your mental approach and whether it is working for you. Find someone you trust, who cares about you, and who is willing to be honest about your blind spots. Another creative way to get feedback is to watch videos of competitors who are tactically different from you, such as those from older eras. Instead of dismissing them as "old-school," ask yourself what might apply to your own training.

3. **Reflect**: Perhaps the most important thing you can do to achieve Extreme Balance is **think**. Challenge yourself by calling your preconceived notions into question, and really think about what you do, what you think, how you perform,

and how you can become more flexible in your thinking. If you find yourself automatically dismissing feedback or reflexively defending yourself when someone gives you feedback, that's often a sign that you have room to grow in that area. We've added a few prompts in the next section that you can use to help jump-start your thinking. If you do nothing else, try some of these.

4. **Record**: You probably log your training sessions and workouts so you can track your progress and look for patterns—that way you can identify any weaknesses and maximize your strengths. Do the same for your mental evolution. Keep a journal or digital file where you can make notes—whether it's about the prompts below or any other observations you and others have made about yourself. By reviewing what you record over time, you will notice patterns and adjust accordingly.

5. **Wrestle**: You will need to do plenty of mental maneuvering to change the way you think. It's OK to wrestle with your thoughts, internal conflicts, or attempts to go against your nature—the process will help you understand how an Extreme Balance mindset can help you develop into a champion. The Spanish term for wrestling is *la lucha*, which means "the struggle," and the mental wrestling you must do can be as difficult a struggle at times as the physical one. But it can have huge payoffs if you're willing to fight for it.

Extreme Balance Prompts

We recommend you record your answers to the following eight questions, revisiting them as often as you like. Even if you don't write them down, it's still a valuable exercise to think about the answers.

1. Think about the paradoxes outlined in the previous chapters, which are listed below. Identify where you fall on a line drawn between the extreme sides of these approaches. You can even do it visually by marking an X to indicate where on the line you see yourself. For example, do you tend to err on the side of caring deeply rather than keeping it in perspective? If so, you would land farther on the left-hand side. If, however, you tend to minimize the importance of your sport or vocation, you would land on the right.

Caring Deeply	◀ · · · · · · · · ▶	Keeping It in Perspective
Focusing on the Process	◀ · · · · · · · · ▶	Focusing on the Outcome
Thinking You're Good Enough	◀ · · · · · · · · ▶	Thinking You're Never Good Enough
Respecting Your Opponent	◀ · · · · · · · · ▶	Crushing Your Opponent
Preparing for Everything	◀ · · · · · · · · ▶	Expecting the Unexpected
Using Your Head	◀ · · · · · · · · ▶	Using Your Instinct
Pushing Through Pain	◀ · · · · · · · · ▶	Pulling Back On the Reins
Being an Individual	◀ · · · · · · · · ▶	Being a Team Player

2. Identify the most extreme mindset in one of the above areas—the place where the X is closest to one end of the spectrum. Think of a time you demonstrated that mindset (for example, an incident in training when you were injured and ended up injuring yourself even more by refusing to take it easy). Now imagine sliding the X to the other end of the spectrum. How does that change the scenario? We call this embracing the "non-slippery slope." Just because you employ the opposite mindset in a specific situation doesn't mean you must take that path forever. You're free to experiment with new mindsets without risking your core values.

3. Identify a paradoxical principle from the above list where your current mindset may have hurt you. Perfectionism, for example, can be helpful in training because that mindset can make good competitors great, but perfectionism in competition can lead to anxiety, hesitation, and overly critical self-talk, which can be counterproductive. Think of that tangible time in your life when your mindset may have worked against you. Next, consider how you might adopt the opposite mindset – or moderate your approach – to find greater balance.

4. How open-minded or close-minded are you about your mindset in each area? Does changing "how you think" change "who you are"?

5. After a bad training session or competition, think about what went wrong. Once you identify the problem, ask yourself if a change in mindset could have led to a different result. How might another approach have worked in your favor?

6. What is the value of "play" as opposed to "work" in your training? Can you think of ways to integrate less stressful training periods and open yourself up to new ways of thinking?

7. If you could ask an opponent how they would beat you, what would they say? Don't just consider the physical component—what would they say about the mental factor?

8. What athletes do you most admire? What have you read or heard about their mental approach that resonates with you? Is it different from the way you think?

These prompts are not one and done. You can think about them often—weekly, monthly, or any time frame you like. Remember, thinking and reflecting is a key component to developing your mental skills. We can't promise that you can pull off a psychological reversal and immediately become someone you're not. But in our experience working with elite athletes, the victories on the mat or in the ring happen once you face the biggest battles in your head.

— ACKNOWLEDGMENTS —

Bruce Babashan

Jurica Barac

Chase Coffman

Ilias Diakomihalis

Yianni Diakomihalis

Mark Ellis

Dan Gable

Nick Gallo

Nick Garone

Keith Gavin

Jay Jackson

Dr. Michael Johnson

Rob Koll

Dr. Anna Lembke

Paul McBeth

Kristin Meek

Sam Meek

Gerald Meerschaert

Dominique Moceanu

Megan Moulton-Levy

Lara Pence

Patrick Regan

Martin Sinković
Valent Sinković
Tiffany Smiley
Ryan Warner
Chris Weidman

— INDEX —

Printed in the USA
CPSIA information can be obtained
at www.ICGtesting.com
JSHW011156250924
70380JS00002B/2